TALES
from
WALES

Dedicated to V.H.P.

TALES
from
WALES

by
LEO DAMANT

A VALLEN PUBLICATION

Vallen Publishers, West Beach, Adelaide

© 1983 Leo Damant

ISBN 0 949406 00 7

Printed at Griffin Press Limited, Marion Road, Netley, South Australia.

Acknowledgements

Ethel Hodder, Shirley Packham, Liz Kahn, Rose Henley, Susie Dean Hunt, Audrey Hirst, Mary Rees. (The Damant Encouragement Award.)

R. Ieuan Edwards, County Librarian, The Hayes, Cardiff, & Harry West, Head Librarian, *Western Mail*, Cardiff, for research material on the Harold Jones murder trials.

Geoff Hopkins & Neil Merkel. Geoff for information on how to do it, Neil for invaluable assistance in bringing the project to a successful conclusion.

Contents

Foreword
Preface

Foreword

Leo Damant is the pseudonym of Leonard Phillips, a Bargoed born Welshman, who has lived in Australia for nearly twenty years. He was fifteen years old when he left the coal tipped valley of the Rhymney for Weston-super-Mare where his family set up business in the hotel industry. He has been many things to many men; salesman, distributor of groceries to chain stores and in his early days a boxing promoter. He even boxed professionally for a time but, with the Welshman's instinct for survival, surrendered that talent to expediency after one win and one loss. Not for him the cauliflower ear, flattened nose and addled wit. He has been a sports writer also and at one time, in the early days of Australian commercial television, with his partner, Jim Bland, wrote gags for comedy shows.

TALES FROM WALES is his first published book, no discredit for a man in his early sixties. It is a volume of short stories recalling life in Wales during the thirties. I first read them with a certain amount of scepticism. Could life have been as simple and as uncomplicated as Leo Damant would have us believe? The answer is yes, in spite of depression and dole queues, poverty and despair; therein lies their charm. Hope is never far away. The human spirit remains to be challenged while the foibles of human nature make sure that it is.

Leo Damant offers no concession to literary style and that is refreshing. His stories are what the title makes them out to be, tales, human interest stories in the best newspaper sense, anecdotes, which is what the short story is about, to relate a clearly defined event within a limited space. Damant's model has been the work of the American short story writer, O. Henry; at his best one of the great masters of the short story form. O. Henry introduced the 'surprise' or 'twist' ending, a kind of trick writing, I suppose, but effective, ingenious and highly entertaining. He was never a profound writer or given to great insight. His prose was direct and lacked nuance. Nevertheless, his literary skill was an accomplishment to be respected.

Similarly, Leo Damant's work will not bear the kind of scrutiny which many critics and academics employ to hobble talent. He brings considerable compassion and understanding to his characters and a certain light hearted irony. In marked contrast to the solemn, sophisticated style of some of his more erudite contemporaries, he writes with simple awareness. He makes no judgments, unlike Caradog Evans, among the first of the Anglo-Welsh writers to break into the English short story tradition.

Evans wrote about the Welsh people with a sense of anger and frustration and when his stories were published they were greeted with hysterical contempt. Evans attacked the bleak side of Welsh life, the hypocrisy of the chapel-going, hymn-singing, money-grabbing, sermon-gasping Welshman, expelling from the chapel unmarried mothers through the main door, while nipping around the back to listen avidly to their woe. This was the Wales Evans despised; the no-give non-conformity which condemned the average Welshman to a life of forced puritanism, formal thrice-Sunday chapel going with prayer meetings mid-week to keep salvation flourishing. Evans was reviled for his heresy and to be found reading his work was command to penitence.

Evans's outrage, in part, was over-reaction to a complex set of historical paradoxes. Wales had been for centuries a bilingual country in which English was a kind of unofficial first language but a cultural second to Welsh. The thirties movement, Urdd Gobaith Cymru (Welsh League of Youth), set out to capitalise the imbalance by claiming that the Welsh language was the one true language of Wales. This movement had been fore-armed by a form of semi-political nationalism at the turn of the century, founded in self-government for Wales: A later political version in the twenties, austere, with sight set on nothing less than statehood with severance from England, also used the Welsh language as a unifying theme. The inspiration for these political and cultural thrusts was the Welsh chapel tradition where only Welsh was spoken and preached from the pulpit, the institution which Caradog Evans, in turn, loathed so heartily.

Growing support for the Welsh language along with nationalist claims manifested itself further when the Royal National Eisteddfod of Wales just after the war, ceased to be a bilingual festival to become a totally Welsh language festival. Today, the historical cycle is strangely complete. Welsh is recognised by English government as an official language and given parity with English in government forms and publications through Office of a Secretary of State for Wales with a seat in cabinet. Even street names are in Welsh and English with income tax forms available in both languages making tax evasion a pretty duel of bilingual wit. It has all been a singular victory for Welsh language patriots: Wales is now truly a bilingual country, as well as musical, with its own national television service in Welsh language.

But it is the non-Welsh speaking Welshman who has been seen to suffer most. Welsh traditionalists tortured him on the rack of identity. As the Welsh language establishment strengthened its hold upon the people of Wales, infiltrating into government and public life, the Welshman without his language, speaking only English, found himself on the outside. It was like being nude without a leaf in sight.

It was never openly stated, of course, but it was conveyed that to be Welsh speaking was a notch up the social scale. Yet, it was not the Welsh politician, serving Wales or Whitehall, or the fervent Welsh rugby fan, singing bread of heaven at Cardiff Arms Park, who brought Wales into focus as a country of exceptional individuals. It was the Welshman writing in English who gained entry into the cultural salons of Europe and America. As a written language Welsh had a prestigious historical past; its poetic tradition, next to the Chinese, was the most sophisticated in the civilised world. Paradoxically again, without the success of the Welshman writing in English the Welsh traditionalists in modern Wales might have become just as easily wailing voices on the slopes of Snowdonia.

Richard Hughes, whose output, at times, of one sentence, achieved after careful revision of about a thousand words a day, gained international status as a major novelist with HIGH WIND IN JAMAICA. Richard Llewelyn amassed a pre-war fortune from HOW GREEN IS MY VALLEY. Emlyn Williams, with NIGHT MUST FALL and THE CORN IS GREEN, brought considerable fame and wealth for himself as writer and actor, at the same time, liberating the Welsh instinct and feeling for the theatre, suppressed for decades. Ivor Novello with THE DANCING YEARS and KING'S RHAPSODY monopolised the musical scene in London and New York. After the war Richard Burton was to become the most talked about actor in the world. Dame Edith Sitwell had already pronounced Dylan Thomas as a poetic talent of genius. Gwyn Thomas, a rare human being, with compassion of a St Francis, one of the great humourist writers of the twentieth century, had the power in print to make people laugh as well as convulse an audience with his wit and barb on television and public platforms.

In the art of the short story Welsh writers in English also surpassed themselves. The mood was predominantly Celtic, power for the dark, tapping unconscious rhythms in castle and manor keeps. The tragedy of the Welsh miner was a betrayed Glendower vanishing into the mists of the Welsh mountains. A nonconformist historical past and socialist present became the themes. Gwyn Jones, who encouraged so many Welsh writers in English when editor of THE WELSH REVIEW, was outstanding master of the short story form. Glyn Jones and John Prichard were enormously gifted. Alun Lewis, another writer of exceptional merit, was killed in the war, the only time for the DAILY EXPRESS to banner headline the death of a poet and writer. Alun

Richards continues to write short stories as well as novels and plays and is currently editor of the Welsh anthology of short stories, subsidised by the Arts Council of Great Britain. It is a family of exceptional talent which, I fear, will never rise again, matched by writers in the Welsh language with their own individual insights.

Leo Damant is much the newcomer, a new boy in the Anglo-Welsh school of writers, that disparaging term, once used freely, like Taffy who raided the English border so successfully to become helplessly known as a thief. What Damant's stories lack in urbanity and style are made up in feeling, perception, mellowness, gentle humour and a wry telling.

He is a welcome addition to the family, of whom, at sexist risk, only the patriarchs have been extolled.

HERBERT DAVIES

Preface

People are shaped and affected by events in their childhood in ways which are sometimes not appreciated until middle, or old age. I was with a couple of youngsters, we were all about twelve at the time, and one of them had an air-gun. We were in a wooded area about a mile out of town and the one with the gun took aim, fired, and down came a bird from the branch of a tree, flopping to the ground at our feet, and dying a few moments later.

I wasn't particularly horrified at the time, though I didn't care for it too much. I was far from being the gentle type, if anything I was fairly callous about most things. But after that incident I have never had much stomach for blood sports. Not that I've actively opposed these pursuits during my lifetime. Other people can do what they will and if that's their idea of pleasure, good luck to them. But the sight of that bird dying at my feet put me off killing animals for all time.

Like everyone else I retain memories of child-hood and early adolescence, and since I spent the first fifteen years of my life in a mining town in the Rhymney Valley it is there my mind wanders when I recall my early days.

One of my first passions was boxing. I saw the fights at the local stadium each Saturday night though I don't recall ever paying to go in. The first boxing match I ever saw, and I couldn't have been more than eight or nine at the time, was at a boxing booth. Most Welshmen are instant experts on the sport so I wasn't too long absorb-ing the finer points and from then on I attended the Saturday night boxing shows without fail and saw some wonderful fights over the years.

By this time the boxer who was known as 'The One and Only', and 'The Ghost with the Ham-mer in his Hand', Jimmy Wilde, had long since retired, to become the legend he still is to this day.

The new hero was Cardiff's pride and joy, Jack Petersen, and we followed his ring exploits with the greatest interest. Not that I ever saw Petersen perform in the ring. He fought in the cities, the boxing capitals, London, Cardiff, Leicester, far away from the valley stadium I frequented. For us, it was the local boxers, a tough, reasonably talented bunch, not too well paid, but certainly value for money.

It was a hard way to make a crust, but at a time of widespread poverty, half a loaf was better than none. This passion for the 'noble art' has remained with me ever since and I've seen some great fighters in action in my time.

If Jimmy Wilde disproved the old adage 'a good big 'un will always beat a good little 'un', Jack Petersen proved it had some validity after all. Wilde could dispose of featherweights when he himself could barely reach the flyweight limit. Petersen, on the other hand, should have stayed in the light-heavyweight division. He was the outstanding British heavyweight champion between the wars, but could have won the world title at light-heavyweight. Why he fought the German heavyweight, Walter Neusel, more than once, is something which baffles me. But no matter, he was one of the great ones, and Welsh boxing fans had every reason to be proud of him. Tommy Farr became another champion we could take pride in and his shot at Joe Louis for the world title was a highlight in a great career.

So those were the heroes of my schooldays, the local heroes I saw in action, and the national heroes I read about in newspapers and books. However, at school my passion was rugby. The sport became an obsession and I was impatient to get into the school team. I didn't make it as quickly as I hoped but once in I always made the team thereafter.

My talent for rugby didn't quite match up to my enthusiasm and I was never too crazy about tackling. I had a secret fear of being booted in the head and used all sorts of tactics to make my tackling look good but probably fooled no one.

Further up the valley there was a boy in the Deri School team named Stevens. He was a monster of six feet, bigger by far than any other junior player in the valley. When we played Deri they beat us by fifty-six points to nil. None of us could stop Stevens once he had the ball and a few tries he scored were achieved with him carrying the ball and about ten of our team over the line at the same time.

Soccer also occupied a fair slice of my time. I played with my gang on a piece of waste ground behind the pub. Today I marvel at footballers who can't use the 'open space' because (and perhaps my memory is playing tricks) we used this method of 'working' the ball when I was about twelve years old. Sometimes, especially during the school holidays, we'd play all day, knocking off only for a bite to eat, then returning to keep playing. My 'team' then was Arsenal, and think, this was back in the days when the 'Gunners' defence had Moss in goal, with Male and Hapgood at full back. If you can remember them you go back a very long time.

We played cricket on the same piece of waste ground, and our heroes were the likes of Walter Hammond, Don Bradman, and Harold Larwood. If our cricket gear was primitive our enthusiasm couldn't be faulted.

Apart from our devotion to sport our leisure-time pursuits included singing and stealing, sometimes conducted simultaneously. We'd raid some poor devil's orchard and on the moonlit walk along a lane leading back to town we'd sing the latest on the 'hit parade'. When I was old enough to go along with the boys 'Ramona' and 'Carolina Moon' were favourites.

Our gang would steal anything. My grand-mother ran the local grocery store and her comment, watching us cavorting around, was 'if it's not too hot, it's not too heavy', and as far as we were concerned she wasn't far wrong.

One Christmas when the shopping spree was in full swing we went to the local Emporium to steal a football. We did it, although it was blown up at the time, by stuffing it up my younger brother's shirt, surrounding him, and bustling out. That ball lasted the entire season, or what remained of it, pretty good really when never a day went by that we didn't boot it around on a pitch which was far from perfect. There were more stones than blades of grass. Fortunately, by the time we were about twelve most of us had the sense to alter our ways.

Horse riding, normally the pursuit of the rich, at least in less well-endowed areas, was another of our passions. We, none of us, owned a horse, but they were there for the taking. There were plenty of mountain ponies within easy reach and when the weather was good we'd 'mitch' from school and head for the hills. Saddles were a luxury we could do without and the bridle consisted of a rope from an orange box which made an acceptable halter. Having caught our mount we'd ride until they were ready to drop, then catch another one. Cruel we were, but there was no malice in us and we never actually rode one until it fell to the ground, but a few of them rolled their eyeballs in relief when we let them go.

If the mountain ponies were off wandering in another area we caught the Co-operative milk-float horses. The company may have been co-operative but the horses were not. Magnificent chestnuts, marvellous mounts, but a bit danger-ous to the inexperienced.

Poverty there was all around. Those of us who grew up at the time of the Depression, the General Strike, the hunger marches, retain a fairly keen memory of the whole scene. The Great War was still fresh in everyone's mind and the number of men carrying around, or not carrying around in the case of amputees, evi-dence of that obscene war, was a constant reminder of the hardship people had endured. It was an indignity that they should now have to bear the burden of poverty.

The spirit though, was unquenchable, and to my mind, when I think back to the days of my youth, best illustrated by a bizarre event, the race for men with wooden legs.

This handicap event with a difference took place in the late twenties, starting at the Capel Hotel, Gilfach, and finishing on the local football field about two miles distant. The valley was well served for men with only one leg, mostly war veterans, but also a few miners who had lost a limb in pit accidents.

I can well remember cheering on our local cobbler, Joe Crease, who gave away a few years and perhaps forty pounds in weight, or over-weight, because the winner was a young war veteran who romped home clear by a half mile and waved his wooden leg in a victory salute.

The environment, itself a casualty of the industrial activity since the middle of the nine-teenth century, was, by the time I arrived on the scene, a disaster area. Overlooking the valley, the Aberbargoed tip stood out like a black volcano, and minor tips dotted the valley and polluted the little river until it looked like a stream of molten tar. The steam, smoke and fumes from the coke-ovens hung around for days when the weather was balmy and at night the sky lit up like a tropical sunset from the steelworks further up the valley.

Coal was used for home heating and fine Clydesdales pulled the carts along the lanes and the coal was dropped outside the back gates of the customers' houses. Ten bob a ton was the going rate and small boys competed for the privilege of carrying the coal into the coal cellar. It was a shilling earned the hard way.

If at first the havoc wrought by industry was an affront to the eyes of the people, time dulled the senses, and they came to accept the scenery for what it was. The tips became playgrounds for venturesome youth and some of their antics were positively lunatic. The overhead coal-buckets which daily added hundreds of tons to the tips were used as a very risky form of transport from one hill to another, hanging underneath like monkeys from a tree, and hoping the bucket wouldn't tilt over to deposit the hanger-on and the load of coal sixty feet to the ground below.

This then was the valley, my home and playground until my family left Wales when I was fifteen years old. For a long time I missed it sorely, the place and the people. Fortunately one has had the pleasure of returning many times, and without fail there is always the same warmth, the same sense of coming home.

They still keep a welcome in the valley.

1 *The Remains of Jimmy Wadlow*

I returned to the valley on a hot day in August and things seemed much the same in regard to the people, except for the fact that they were twenty years older, or the fact that some of them were dead.

'How's old so and so?' I'd ask.

'Oh, he's dead and buried.' Always the 'and buried'. In the valley, it seemed, being dead was just not enough. They had to be buried as well, just to make it positive.

I hadn't noticed this before whilst I'd lived there, but at least a half dozen enquiries were met with this response. Ness Reynolds, an old friend of the family, agreed that he himself used the expression and being used to it didn't see anything strange in it.

'But it is true,' he said. 'We do say, "and buried".'

I should have known better than to make a point of it, this little discovery of mine, because before long I was asking about somebody else. Jimmy Wadlow. Jimmy had been a colleague of mine, him an old hand, and me a new boy in the advertising office of a departmental store.

'How's old Jimmy Wadlow?' I asked, fearing the worst.

'Dead.' Ness spoke with a finality which was almost as good as 'and buried'.

'And buried?' I enquired.

'Two halves, best bitter,' Ness said to Walter the barman.

'I remember your father well,' Walter said, pushing the beer over to us. 'Lovely pianist. Nice chap. Oh yes, I remember Harry all right.'

We walked over to a table, Ness leading the way. He was big, Ness, bulky, and I could see he'd want to take the weight from his feet. He was known to just about everyone in the valley because he'd been an insurance collector for years before his promotion to manager.

We sat down and had a sip of the beer. We were in the Working Men's Club, Sunday, getting towards noon, and it was beginning to fill up. Ness looked at the man on the next table, walked over to him and had a brief, though earnest discussion. I assumed Ness was doing the old routine of telling a client his policy would lapse if he didn't get some money into the office.

He returned to the table. 'Got to keep on top of 'em,' he said to me. 'Now, where were we?'

'Jimmy Wadlow. You were saying he was dead. You didn't say "and buried".'

Ness held up his hand. 'In a minute. About Walter. Yes, he did know your father really well. Had a good voice, Walter. Boy soprano. Your father helped him a lot. The voice never the same after it broke. Still quite good though.'

'Jimmy Wadlow?' I persisted.

'Yes, I didn't say "and buried",' he agreed.

I waited. He took a fair sip of his beer and sat holding the glass in his hand, thinking. There was some activity going on on the small stage in preparation for the usual Sunday display of local talent.

'Not buried,' Ness said, 'and for good reason.'

I was becoming impatient. Ness was the most fluent of speakers, as one would expect from a man who had sold thousands of pounds' worth of policies, served many years on the district council, and was a popular speaker in debating societies up and down the valley.

'Africa.' Ness said. He bit his bottom lip and looked absently at the faces of the other drinkers dotted around the club room.

'What about Africa?' I asked.

'Well, Jimmy's only offspring . . . you remember his daughter Maggie? She married a bloke who emigrated to South Africa. Then Maggie joined him. So poor Jimmy was all alone. His wife was dead by this time . . . and of course, buried.' He nodded with satisfaction at having beaten me to it. 'And Jimmy, poor devil, really missed Maggie. He cried, wept like a baby after she left. Pathetic, it was, but easily understood.

I'm a father myself and I'd hate the idea of any of mine going that far away. Not seeing the grandkids. No, cruel that.'

Ness turned to the chap he'd been talking to on the next table. He called over to him. 'Just telling Leo about Jimmy Wadlow. Terrible, wasn't it?'

The man shook his head, sorrowfully. 'Terrible,' he said. 'Yes, terrible.' He looked at me then. 'Oh, so that's Leo, is it? Knew your father well, Leo. Lovely touch, lovely.'

I nodded but the man's name escaped me. 'Why terrible?' I asked Ness. 'Good God, what happened to him?'

'Yes, you wouldn't think it could happen to a man born and bred in the valley. Usually they die from all sorts of things but certainly not that.'

There was no rushing him and I finished my beer and went to the bar for a couple more. When I returned Ness was filling and lighting his pipe so I sat and waited.

Finally he said: 'After a while Jimmy decided to go out to South Africa and visit them. Actually, and he told me this himself, he was going with the express purpose of persuading them to come back home. He felt he was too old to settle in another country himself and life wasn't worth living without Maggie and the three grandchildren around. Some people are like that. Very close. Very dependent on the family. Only natural.'

'Cheers,' I said, sipping the beer.

'Your good health, my son,' Ness said, taking an outsize swig. 'Haaaah! That's a drop of first rate brew. First rate. He knows his stuff, Walter.'

'Never mind Walter. What about Jimmy?'

Ness shook his head, slowly. 'Ridiculous really,' he said. He called over to the chap on the next table. 'I was just saying about what happened to Jimmy . . . ridiculous, don't you think?'

The chap shook his head. 'Just ridiculous,' he agreed. 'Quite ridiculous.'

Ness turned and fixed me with a penetrating stare. 'You sure you haven't heard this story before? Never?'

'Honest to God, Ness. I didn't even know Jimmy was dead, never mind how it happened.'

'Well, the bare facts are as follows. Jimmy finally got away to South Africa to see his daughter. Oh, he was excited all right.' He called over to the chap on the next table again. 'Excited, wasn't he? Jimmy? Before he left for South Africa?'

'Oh, very,' the bloke said. 'Very excited. Beside himself, you could say.'

'Yes, he was. Beside himself,' Ness concurred. 'And then it happened. One minute he was here, the next minute we had the news from Maggie about the tragedy. After he'd been there a couple of weeks he decided to see something of the country. I expect he felt he might be getting underfoot, as it were. So he went on this tour, by coach, as I recollect. A small coach, about a dozen passengers, and they were in the famous lion reserve up North and they had a breakdown. They were told to stay near the coach but Jimmy didn't. That's when it happened. Tragedy.'

'What? Killed by a lion?'

'Exactly. Happened in a flash. Not a hundred yards from the coach. They tried to drive the lion off but within minutes there were half a dozen of 'em at him. The passengers were helpless and after the lions came the vultures and jackals or hyenas or whatever they are and that was the end of poor old Jimmy. Cor, what a way to go! Gives me the creeps.'

I shook my head sympathetically. 'You said it, Ness. Not nice. Not nice at all.'

'I'm surprised you didn't ask about the carcass, the skeleton, the frame?'

'Who cares?' I asked, 'When you're dead, you're dead.'

'True enough,' Ness agreed. 'But you it was who raised the point about the Welsh always saying dead, and buried.'

'Yes, but what about it? It's a figure of speech. Something I noticed. A peculiarity. A Welsh idiom. I certainly didn't notice it when I lived here. In Jimmy's case you could say dead and devoured. Poor devil.'

'Yes. I must agree again,' replied Ness. 'But in this case there are peculiar circumstances.'

'I can't wait,' I said.

'Yes,' Ness went on, 'Peculiar to this case, because one of the passengers was a medical student, and he wanted a skeleton, and he gathered up the bones, sorted them out, and used Jimmy to help his anatomical studies. When he qualified to practice medicine he donated Jimmy's skeleton to the college and to this very day a Welshman is there, helping students, black and white, in their quest for medical knowledge. And that's why I couldn't say "and buried".'

I controlled myself for about ten seconds then laughed in Ness's face.

He looked pained.'Let's have a little decorum,' he said. 'Just a little respect.'

A man had entered the club. He looked over at me, smiled, and gave a wave of recognition. I walked over and shook hands with him. 'Really great to see you, Jimmy,' I said. 'Go over and sit with Ness. I'll get you a drink.'

I walked to the bar. 'Two halves of best bitter, please Walter,' I said. 'And a glass of coconut juice for Jimmy.'

2 Serenade

'How many miles have you walked, then?' the lady asked.

'Well, it must be close to seventy,' the man said. He had removed his shoes and socks and sat at the edge of the pavement with his feet in the gutter.

'Seventy miles!' the woman said. She poured him another cup of tea from the urn and added the milk. 'Help yourself to sugar, m'dear.'

The roadside stop had been well organised and the few hundred men in the group had all had a meal and a few cups of tea. When they'd finished eating most of them lit up a cigarette, and they sat around the street, weariness evident in the lean, gaunt faces, and for the most part they were quiet.

'It was nice talking to you,' the man said. He pulled on his shoes and socks and stood up. Cigarette ends were tossed into the gutter and they stirred, en masse, and then lined up in a column of fours. Marshalls walked up and down, talking at them, laughing, and stirring them back to life.

They started then, on another stretch of the long walk to London, and from their throats and their hearts they began to sing the songs of the land of their birth.

The lady on the tea-urn had tears in her eyes as the bedraggled mob moved on. Their gratitude to the ladies of the little Gloucestershire village had been polite, shy almost, and her heart ached for them, these men from the valleys parading their poverty and despair.

'Well, them Welshies can certainly sing,' her neighbour said.

'Such lovely voices.'

'Ah, but will it do any good, m'dear? That's what I want to know?'

'The one I was talking to, he said, "they call us hunger marchers ... but really we're job marchers ... we're the blight on society's conscience. There's no dignity in not having a job. If this form of government can't give us the opportunity to live with dignity there's another one waiting to move in."'

'Yer ... oi d'wonder what he means by that?'

'Well, I don't know m'dear. It bent much to ask for. Everybody ought to have a job ... something. Just listen to that singing. Poor buggers.'

3 *The Man Who Knew Secrets*

His name was Tommy Harding but they called him Tom Peep. He walked the hills with his binoculars and knew all the secrets of the lovers in the long grass in the height of summer. He knew the names of the married women who met furtive strangers from the far ends of the valley and the business men in cars who drove their secretaries and shop assistants to secluded spots along the lanes. He never talked about his knowledge but put it to use in other ways.

Times were hard and Tom Peep had not been gainfully employed for over two years. Now he was in business for himself. The business of silence.

His excuse for roaming the countryside was a sleek greyhound, once a champion, which through injury would never race again. He claimed he was building up its stamina to return it to the track. The dog had cost him nothing and he grew fond of it as they spent their hours together in his search for more knowledge.

It all began with Mrs Lilian Day, teacher of pianoforte, big in the chapel, husband a deacon, no children, nice house on Marble Street up the hill from the Palace Cinema. Mrs Lilian Day was a full-breasted matron of almost forty years of age and she loved young boys. It was her weakness, her passion, and she had ample opportunity to nourish it. What healthy fifteen year old boy could hold out for long when Mrs Day put her arms around him from behind to demonstrate correct fingering whilst her marvellous breasts caressed the back of his neck?

She teased, tickled, and rewarded good work with squeezes and little kisses and hardly believing their luck her little boy pupils responded by exploring her fulsome charms with groping, inexperienced hands.

One wet and windy night when she hadn't quite managed to seduce a new pupil she decided to drive him the few hundred yards to his home.

'I'll drop young Griffiths off home and get some fish and chips on the way back, my love.' She made the announcement to her husband who was sitting in the kitchen.

'Shsh,' he replied. 'Listenin' to this play on the wireless. Very good it is, very good. Yes, yes, all right.'

And they climbed into her little Ford and Tom Peep saw what happened when the car stopped at the end of the deserted street because he lived close by and was on his way home.

It took him a week to work up his courage to call on Mrs Day and he found her in the garden, weeding around the flower beds. He told her what he knew and suggested she might like a real man instead of a young boy and received a rude shock when she stood up, her face cold like a mask, eyes full of contempt.

She assured him he was nothing better than an out and out waster, her husband was ten times the man and she didn't want him or any other grown man for that matter. She gave him a pound note and told him that if he breathed a word she would personally ram a carving-knife up his wind-pipe.

'I'll keep quiet,' he assured her. 'But I'll be back in a month. Let's say I'm doin' a bit of gardening.'

He learned quickly, was merciless to the vulnerable, and his fortunes improved rapidly. He developed a number of techniques, sometimes the telephone, often the direct frontal attack. In company, but just out of earshot, he would say to a prospective victim ... . 'Oh Mr Morgan, didn't I see you parked in Angel Lane last Tuesday evening with Mrs ....' This, in a stage whisper was often enough to start money changing hands.

He was devious, cunning, and quite single minded as he searched out the wrong-doers. He was threatened frequently, and learned soon enough that there were some too influential to cross. But, in the valley, there was enough sin to ensure a steady flow of money.

Then, on a warm June evening, he made his first big mistake. The new Armstrong parked on a quiet part of the mountain road belonged to Watkins the greengrocer, and he knew Watkins was up to no good. A man and woman were in the car and Tom Peep jumped to the wrong conclusion.

His direct approach to Watkins some days later was met with a puzzled frown. Watkins left the saloon bar where Tom Peep had accosted him and on arriving at home had proceeded to give his wife a severe battering. Finally she confessed that she had been in the car, which Watkins had taught her to drive only a few weeks before, with a lover, one Otto James, a commercial traveller.

Watkins, intending to make things as difficult as possible for his wife's lover, telephoned the James household, hoping to get Mrs James on the line. Otto however, answered the phone and said his wife was in Newport for a few days, visiting her sick sister. Watkins cursed him then, told him what a stinking cur he was, and assured him that at the earliest opportunity he would inform Mrs James of her husband's infidelity.

The following day Otto James wandered in a daze along the lane which skirted the railway siding. After a sleepless night, Otto, frantic with worry about what his wife, now seven months pregnant was about to learn from Watkins, turned off the lane and absently walked along the side of the railway track.

Tom Peep was prowling the same area and his greyhound had just chased a rabbit from the edge of the reservoir and lost it in the thick grass near the fence which ran along the side of the railway track. He spotted James, hopped over the fence and shouted out a greeting.

'Hello Otto. Taking a stroll, is it?'

James didn't reply but he stopped and stared vacantly at Tom Peep. A train was approaching, the Cardiff stopper, making its leisurely way up through the valley, and as it drew close Otto James threw himself under the wheels and died screaming as Tom Peep stood there, his helpless shriek of horror drowned by the clacking of the wheels on the steel track.

There are few real secrets in the valley. The police had long had their eye on Tom Peep and in his state of shock he admitted to being a blackmailer. They assumed that Otto James was one of his victims and that Tom Peep had killed him.

That was why, on a freezing January morning in 1930, they hanged him in Cardiff gaol. Outside the prison gates stood a stout lady in a fur coat. She held a banner which read: ABOLISH CAPITAL PUNISHMENT.

4 *Lights Out*

It was Friday and Mary went into the Cut-Price Stores with her mother to get a few things for the week-end. Even though Mary was married now, her mother still did all the talking. That was the way it had always been and Mary just stood there, her mother busy around the store, peering at this and that and talking the whole time.

'Hello Mrs Tucker,' the lady behind the counter said.

'Cheese fresh is it? Looks nice and what about the bacon? Can you cut it thick. Mick likes it thick. Thicker the better. You got any pickled walnuts, he likes the way you do 'em, Mrs Dix? It's colder today, the Labour Exchange is coming along well almost finished. Good position here, you knew what you were doing, good head on your shoulders, I always said that. And tinned tomatoes, our Mary was saying those eggs last week were the best since our hens stopped laying. Can't get

15

fresh anywhere 'round here except you, but you go to Abergavenny market an' it's well worth it.'

'Tea,' Mary said.

'And tea. Typhoo,' said Mrs Tucker. 'An' Ideal Milk because I can't keep him in fruit salad but I don't want any of that because I got tinned pears for Sunday tea. Have you got any of that H.P. sauce yet you were out last week? Or I don't mind Daddies. Nice pickled onions but I do my own.'

'When's your Stanley coming home, Mary?' Mrs Dix wanted to know.

'Tonight,' Mary replied. 'Just for the week-end.'

'And then he's going to the China station?' Mrs Dix said. 'China! How long will the Navy keep him there?'

'Three years.'

'Three years! Good God, that's not much of a married life!'

'When people d'say that,' Mrs Tucker butted in, 'I d'tell 'em to mind their own business. Navy men make good husbands.'

'Course they do, Mrs Tucker,' Mrs Dix replied. 'Very good. But I was thinking about Mary. Not easy, I shouldn't think.'

'That's all Mrs Dix. How much do I owe you?'

Mrs Tucker walked from the store, with Mary carrying the bag of groceries.

'This is heavy. You should have asked Mr Dix to deliver,' Mary complained.

When they arrived home she dropped the bag

of shopping and rubbed her shoulder. 'Oh Mum, I feel as if I've pulled something.'

'Where's that stepfather of yours? He's never here when he's wanted.'

'He said he'd have to go to the club-rooms today. Big match tomorrow, so he says. They're playing Maesteg and they've got a lot of injuries from last week.'

'I'll injure him when I see him. Left this house like a pig-stye. Never folds a newspaper or empties an ash-tray. Men!'

'Why doesn't Mick get a regular job, Mum. Drawing the dole and making a bit as a masseur for the rugby club's all right but I like the idea of steady money.'

'That's right, my girl, but Mick's well known. There's a lot who send for him to visit and Doctor Dan sends patients he doesn't want to bother with. Aches and pains. Good money in it. I never said, I know, but Mick does all right. He's pretty crafty about money Mick is, and no-one the wiser.'

'Well, if he's any good he'd better cure this shoulder of mine because I think I've pulled something. Like a toothache.'

Mrs Tucker put the groceries away into her pantry and did a swift tidy up around the sitting room. She sat down then and lit a Woodbine.

They sat across the table from each other drinking the tea which Mary carried in from the kitchen. Mrs Tucker talked in bursts, rapid, gossipy, knowing all the local slander and repeating it with great relish. In the middle of one of her monologues the young sailor walked in. His pink, chubby face beamed.

'Any tea left in that pot?' He dropped his kit-bag, leant over the table and kissed Mary on the cheek.

'Hello Stanley, my lovely,' Mrs Tucker said. 'You're early.'

'You get it, Mum,' Mary said. 'My shoulder's sore.'

'Oh, what you done, my love?' asked Stanley.

'You're home then?' Mary greeted him.

'Yes,' the young sailor said, ruefully. 'Last time for a long time.'

'It'll pass,' called out Mrs Tucker from the kitchen. 'And our Mary'll be waiting for you . . . waiting for the ship to come in.' She laughed as though she'd made a good joke.

'Shall we go to the pictures tonight?' Stanley looked at his wife. 'I saw on the placards there's a good one at the Palace. Musical. I like musicals.'

'I like a good drama,' Mrs Tucker said, handing Stanley his tea.

'My shoulder's sore. I don't think I could sit through the pictures.'

Mary's step-father came in then and sat at the table with them. He was a fit-looking man, approaching middle age, blue, keen eyes and a shock of greying hair.

'What's the matter with your shoulder, Mary?'

'Carrying groceries. Strained it.' Mary's mother didn't give her a chance to reply.

'Oh, so you're a diagnostician now, are you?' Mick said. 'However, this time you might be right. On the other hand you could be wrong.'

He walked around the table and grasped Mary's wrist. He moved her arm gently, waiting for some reaction from her.

'Oh!' Mary moaned, her face expressing pain.

Mick was talking softly as he worked, a soothing sympathetic note in his voice, but letting the others know they were listening to an expert. 'In this region we have the muscles of the shoulder girdle ... trapezius ... infraspinatus ... triceps ... pectoral ... deltoids ... the question is, naturally enough, which of the many groups of muscles have been damaged? See, the difference between your ordinary rubber-downer and the expert manipulator is the ability to select different groups of muscles and treat them properly. You not only have to know where they are ... but what they do ... right, take that blouse off.'

Mary removed her blouse and sat modestly trying to cover her generous bosom with her good arm, but Mick, seeming oblivious to the hillocks of flesh, kneaded and probed and Mary gave a shriek of pain as Mick emitted a triumphant 'Aah!'

'Ligament,' Mick said. 'When you carry things don't take the weight on an outstretched arm. Wasn't much trouble. Displaced. I just flipped it back.' He held up his hands. 'A genius,' he said.

'Oh, thank you Mick. It feels a bit better.'

The week-end went by and on the Monday

morning they all saw Stanley off at the station. He was quite tearful as he left and Mrs Tucker was visibly moved.

'We'll be waiting, my lovely,' she cried out, having the last word as the train pulled away.

Mary took the whole thing in her stride and carried on with her job at the Emporium. Stanley's allotment was paid regularly and she saved all of it. She could see the beginning of a substantial nest egg.

He wrote often, long ardent letters and Mary wrote less frequently, factual accounts of where she went, what happened at work, which movies she saw, and how much money she was saving.

Stanley sent photographs of himself and his shipmates posing off-duty on the deck of the cruiser. Mary sent him snaps of her mother and Mick in the garden and also little candid-camera shots from Swansea and Barry Island where they often spent a pleasant day at the seaside.

They lived quite close to the Emporium where Mary worked and sometimes she went home for lunch. One day Mick was there alone, her mother having taken off to visit a friend in hospital. Mick, having had an eyeful of Mary's lovely bosom during the shoulder treatment was pleasantly surprised when she told him they were doing stock-taking at the shop and had felt pains in her shoulder that very morning.

Mick rubbed her shoulder sympathetically. Mary slipped out of her blouse and looked up at him with an expression which called for more of his expert attention and once again he found himself looking down at her marvellous cleavage. He probed around her shoulder and tried to look professional, objective.

She felt better after a few minutes and smiled gratefully at him. He gave her shoulder the customary pat to indicate it was all done and then gave her breasts a swift caress.

'Lovely,' he said.

She looked down at herself. 'Too big, really.'

'Nonsense, my love.' Mick was breathing rather quickly now. 'Men love 'em. I'll bet Stanley appreciates 'em?'

'Maybe. But I didn't give him much opportunity.'

'Good God! And he's your husband.

'Too clumsy,' Mary told him. 'I didn't really like him touching me.'

'Poor Stanley.' He slipped his hand into her cleavage and massaged the nipples gently. 'Proper massage could reduce them nicely but why spoil a good thing? Still, if that's what you want come up to the bedroom.' Mick went from the room and up the stairs, and Mary, after hesitating briefly, followed him.

Some months later they left the village together and Mrs Tucker was all alone. The gossip was ferocious but she held her head high and refused to discuss it or mention either of them by name, but alone in the house she cried bitter tears and read and re-read the brief note Mary had left her.

Stanley came home, a bemused, brown-skinned naval man, still chubby and looking no older. He had cocoa with his mother-in-law and she told him the story.

She didn't know where they were and didn't intend finding out. If he found them she didn't wish to know about it. He could sleep in Mary's old bed tonight, she said, because it was late, but tomorrow he would have to go.

She went to bed and left him. Stanley sat there for a long time and finally went from the kitchen and up the stairs.

A light under the door told him she was not yet asleep and he knocked on the door.

'Come in Stanley,' she called out. 'What do you want?'

'I don't know what to do,' Stanley said, hopelessly. 'It isn't as if I had a family. I'm all alone, really.' He sat at the side of the bed. 'Why do you keep the light on? All these books . . . do you read all night?'

'Sometimes,' she said.

'Oh, I can understand. A shock, it was.'

'No, it's not that, my love. When my first husband died . . . Mary's father that is . . . terrible it was. Died in the night. I woke up and his arms were around me and he was cold, dead. Oh, gives me the shudders. So, until I married Mick, twelve months later, I always kept the light on. Afraid of the dark I was. Never told anybody. Afraid I am, again.'

'Oh, poor Mam,' Stanley said. 'Never mind, I'll

sit by here and you can go to sleep and not be afraid.'

'It's cold in bed tonight,' Mrs Tucker said.

'I'll fix that,' Stanley said, taking off his jumper. He climbed into the bed and buried his face in her bosom.

'There, there,' said Mrs Tucker. 'Put the light out, there's a good boy.'

5 Gang Warfare

The Pengam gang were affronted. One of their members had been given a hiding and a couple of others smacked about a bit and when the victims related what had happened the others were very annoyed.

Billy Smythe was seventeen and the nearest thing to a leader they had. He wasn't anxious to get involved with the Gelligaer lot because there were some hard ones there. Billy wasn't noted for his fistic ability, brain power being his forte, having had twelve months in the Grammar before his Dad kicked him out of it and made him go underground.

It seemed that Georgie Batt, Reg Watkins and Len Ruthers had been at the Saturday night dance and had talked to the wrong girls because about five toughs jumped them as they were walking back to Pengam and poor Georgie had come off worst.

'Don't come back,' their attackers advised them.

So, on Sunday morning, when the shock of seeing Georgie's battered features was fresh in their minds they resolved to round up a few of the boys and pay a visit to Gelligaer and sort a few of them out. The word spread and they looked to Billy to come up with a plan of campaign.

At this turn of events Billy's brain turned to jelly and he was wishing he'd been born at another time in history, but he kept quiet, and silence as we know is often a good substitute for wisdom.

Finally, realising there was a limit to how long he could remain mute, Billy pointed to Georgie and said: 'I don't think Georgie should come. You've had enough, Georgie.' he added.

Georgie protested vigorously. 'I'll come all right. I been lying awake all night thinking about what I'm going to do to those rotten sods. I'll kill the buggers!'

So the plan evolved to go to Gelligaer, small groups split up from the ten who wanted to go, and when the enemy was sighted, swift attacks, no boots, fight fair unless the others started the rough stuff, then back to Pengam and obscurity. The enemy, all adolescents, girl crazy, would be on the prowl trying to pick up crumpet in the Sunday afternoon streets in their Sunday best, or in the park or the Italian cafe.

Then Georgie's brother informed them that

Georgie wasn't feeling too well and had gone to bed. At two o'clock they headed off, emergency arms such as short hunks of wood down the legs of some trousers, one with a length of chain around the neck, inside the shirt, and one or two with home-made knuckle-dusters.

They paraded around for an hour but of the enemy not a sight. They were getting the eye from the Gelligaer girls and soon it became difficult to remember what they came for.

Then Millie Forde, big-busted, brazen, walking with her friend Rosie Martin, saw the hunk of wood in Billy's trousers. She nudged Rosie and they stared, eyes wide with astonishment.

'Good God! Did you see that?' Millie gasped. 'He's abnormal!'

Rosie didn't reply but stopped and turned in her tracks, her eyes following the boys' progress down the street.

Billy, walking, hobbling really, with Len Ruthers, had noted Rosie's interest and they passed the girls, did an about-turn a hundred yards down the street and went after them.

'Going for a walk?' Billy asked them.

'We are walking,' Rosie replied, 'Though how you can walk is a mystery to me.'

And soon the two couples were in a field on the way to the mountainside and a pleasant afternoon followed. The same fate befell most of the other avengers and they drifted back to Pengam in ones and twos and threes and as they arrived they heard the news that the Gelligaer boys had paid a visit to Pengam and the only one of the Pengam gang they found was Georgie, feeling better later in the afternoon, had gone to the shop for a packet of Woodbines and ran smack into the enemy and they'd given him what for.

Billy was deposed as leader forthwith but he didn't care because he'd found Rosie and in the fullness of time they were married in Gelligaer and quite a few of the old Gelligaer gang were at the wedding.

If Rosie was ever disappointed with Billy as a lover she never said, though once she knitted him a cardigan and when he tried it on it was about six sizes too big.

6 *Harold*

(On 5th February, 1921, Freda Burnell, aged 8½ years, of 9, Earl Street, Abertillery, South Wales, was murdered in a shed used as a warehouse. Her body was found in a lane behind Duke Street in the same area.

A sixteen year old youth, Harold Jones, was arrested and charged with the crime. At Monmouthshire Assizes, 21st June, 1921, he was aquitted.

Shortly afterwards, Flora Little, aged 9, of 4, Darren Road, Abertillery, disappeared.)

They were dead now and that was that. He could remember the smell. First the body smell, sweet, and the breath, hot, then the petticoat, rustling, and the legs in the stockings, and garters. White flesh, blue knickers. She knew she was going to die, the first one, and would have screamed blue murder and she tried but couldn't, mouth opening soundless then he silenced her good. Freda, 8½.

Then the other one and harder too. People near. Flora, 9.

Don't think guilty, boy. They'll know soon enough. A week now and still searching, looking, talking, and they know, no hope now.

'What me? Never saw her Sergeant, never. Run away, she has, if you ask me. Flighty. Always was. Certainly I'll come willing. Just have to tell my Mam I'll be gone for a bit.'

'I'll be gone for a bit, Mam, tell Dad I'll come to the Institute with him tonight, just fancy a game of snooker.'

'Well I never, Sergeant! I never thought you brought me here to ask me that! Told you. Never saw her. Not that day or the day before. She's run away, mun. Fancy you asking me that.'

'I never did! I don't care what her father said. I never pulled her knickers down when she was coming from Sunday school.'

'Oooh . . . that's a wicked lie. Wicked. I don't never look in peoples' windows. I go straight home. From the Institute and the pictures and from anywhere.'

'Oh, killed her, is it? Dead she is then? You show me the body then. A body. Then I'll believe it.'

'Oh, so I didn't kill her but I know where the body is? That's a good one.'

'Time to think about it. I don't need no time to think about it. I don't know nothing.'

Keep calm boy. Bluffing they are. Iss cold in here. Locked up indeed. An' Mam cooking tea.

Asked for it they did. Anybody laughs at me I
knows what to do. She's safe there. Looking
forward to that snooker. I bet I'd be another
Walter Lindrum if I practised. Dad says I got the
beating of him already. That Sergeant's a crafty
sod. Who's he think he is? Crafty sod. So I got to
wait for the Inspector. Then he'll let me go, but
you watch your step boy, they're crafty sods so
act innocent, not too indignant, hurt, that's it
hurt. I got to be hurt. But patient. Watch 'em,
they're cute, but I can see through the sods.
Better watch that Inspector when he arrives.
Get's a bit rough, that Sergeant says, so let him.
Keep your mouth shut, boy, shut, or they'll have
you. He's not bad the Sergeant. Don't think he
thinks I done it.

'Look here, Inspector, I think I've told the
Sergeant everything I know. Can't help really, so
if you don't mind I'm playing snooker with my
Dad tonight.'

'Over the whole thing again? Oh, look here,
Inspector, I'm trying to help. It's all written down.
I've said. At nine o'clock that night I was in bed.
Mam and Dad out having a drink, they said, and
I was in bed, reading.'

'Oh, my head, you bastard! You hit me again
and I'll see a solicitor.'

'Thank you Sergeant. I needed a cup of tea.
That Inspector's a disgrace. He's going to get it I
can tell you.'

'Oh, I know. You gotta ask questions. He hurt
me you know. No need for that.'

'Keep me here indefinitely? But it's my birth-day soon. I'll be seventeen.'

'I done my best to find her. I been searching with the others. I been all along the mountain road and down at the river and the reservoir.'

'I know she'd been home for tea. Everybody knows.'

'Ooh! You wait till our Dad hears about this! I told you, mun. I didn't kill her. You don't even know she's dead. Listen, I want to go. Playing snooker with my Dad. My Dad will send you a solicitor's letter.'

'Don't keep calling me Harry. My name's Harold. Harold, that's what my name is, not Harry.'

'What do you mean, I won't be able to live with it? Don't worry about me, boyo.'

'No, I won't confess. Even if I did do it I wouldn't confess. Who wants to be hanged?'

'Oh, they won't hang me. Too young. That's a consolation. Why me? I wouldn't hurt a fly. You ask my Mam. You ask anybody. I never been in a fight in my life.'

'What do you mean by that? I'd rather play with girls, indeed. Who said that? I'll kill 'em.'

'What you putting on your hat for? We going somewhere? I'm not going anywhere 'cept the Institute. With my Dad. Snooker.'

'Taking you to her? Me? I keep telling you. I don't know where she is. How could I take you to her? What's that, a pair of knickers?'

'My Dad gave them to you? My Dad didn't

know where they were. How could he give them to you?'

'All right then. I'll show you where she is. Have to climb up though. She's in the attic.'

'What, three of you coming? She's dead, you know. Won't hurt you.'

'Will it be in the papers? News of the World?'

(Flora Little's body was found in the attic of Harold Jones' home at 10, Darren Road, Abertillery on 9th July, 1921. Harold Jones was again sent for trial and confessed to both crimes. Because of his age, he was sentenced to be detained during His Majesty's pleasure.

Harold Jones served twenty years and was released on licence in 1941. He died in 1971.)

7 Sweets, Chocolates, Cigarettes

Elsie walked from the office of the manager of the Palace cinema in a daze. Her wildest dream had come true. She could start on Monday, the chocolate girl at the cinema, and when the lights went up at the interval and dimmed again, she would be in the spotlight, standing there with the illuminated tray of sweets and chocolates and cigarettes. It was Elsie's idea of stardom and better by far than Woolworths where she had worked since leaving school.

She told everyone and the word spread rapidly. On the Monday of her appearance all her friends and relatives, all the neighbours and near neighbours, were at the Palace for Elsie's debut.

The Palace was one of the town's three cinemas. It had hard seats in the fourpenny's, plush in the sixpenny's, and often the film broke down. During the delay the lights went up and people looked around inquisitively to see who else was in the audience. They called out quite unselfconsciously when they recognised a face.

'Hello Dai. What shift you on next week.' 'What-o Evan boy, where's the Mrs tonight then?'

The people of the valley practically lived in the cinema and film stars occupied quite a slice of most conversations. 'You see Jean Harlow in the pictures last night? Her hair's never that colour.' 'I read in Film Weekly that Laurel and Hardy are going to split up. Gor, they're a funny couple. Our Oscar laughs till he cries. I don't like 'em.'

The 'silents' had been popular but when the 'talkies' came the American accents were a distinct shock. 'They d'talk through their noses. Sound like bloody ducks.'

If the valley audiences were puzzled by the transatlantic intonations they were no less bemused by the plush Mayfair accent of the British stars. 'Hellew dahrling . . . hew lahvleh to see yew . . .' 'Bloody stupid,' was the general opinion.

The two back rows of seats at the Palace were almost as good as a marriage-bed and the snapping of elastic was accompanied by some heavy breathing.

'If you want to hold it it's under my hat.'

'Watch my stockings, I don't want any runs.'

'Have a Park Drive.' 'What for? This place is blue with smoke. Just take deep breaths.'

'Excuse me, would you mind moving over a bit. You're occupying half my seat as well.'

'That's Mrs Pomeroy in the next row. I hope

to God she hasn't seen this picture before or she'll be yelling out what's coming next.'

There was a full house for Elsie's first night at the Palace because they were showing a Gracie Fields picture and the Lancashire singer was a great favourite in the valley. Elsie, feeling tremendously glamorous in her gold-trimmed uniform was waiting for Mr Hopkins, the manager, to give her some final instructions. Everyone, of course, knew Mr Hopkins by sight. Elsie did, and she had a lot of respect for Mr Hopkins. He was stocky, chubby even, with black hair and a ruddy complexion. He always looked ever so smart with his dark suit, white shirt, black tie, and patent leather shoes. He was old, of course, at least thirty-eight or more, but Elsie knew that quite a lot of the girls who went to the Palace really fancied him.

Elsie herself respected Mr Hopkins because she had been in the Palace the night someone shouted 'FIRE' and Billy Jones from Gilfach jumped over six rows of seats and broke all his front teeth. Mr Hopkins, it was, who rushed into the cinema and calmed everybody down.

She'd had some good laughs in the Palace. There was the night the picture starred Duke Wayne, the singing cowboy. After the Duke had sung a song, accompanying himself by strumming his guitar, the old man sitting by the camp-fire on the screen said ... 'Son, I could listen to you all night.' And from the audience someone yelled out, 'Christ, that's more than I could do.' It was Will Davis, a well-known local music teacher.

Mr Hopkins arrived at last and escorted Elsie into his office. There was a sofa against a wall and he sat down and beckoned her to join him.

'Now, come and sit by here, Elsie my lovely.'

She sat, primly, waiting for Mr Hopkins to elaborate on her duties.

'In a minute,' said Mr Hopkins, 'You'll be on. When the spotlight hits you, be ready. Speak up. Say it. Sweets, chocolates, cigarettes . . . Let me hear you say it. C'mon, don't be shy.'

'SWEETS . . . CHOCOLATES . . . CIGARET-TES.' Her voice was clear, strong, and only a slight nervousness was evident.

'Oh, lovely, lovely,' intoned Mr Hopkins. 'Oh, we've made a find here, I can see. A discovery, as they say in Hollywood Now then Elsie . . . apart from the important duties of serving our patrons with refreshments . . . there are other duties . . . important duties also. It has to do with the behaviour of some of our patrons and what goes on in some parts of the auditorium.' Mr Hopkins rested his hand on Elsie's shoulder.

'To say that some of our patrons become amorous during the picture would be putting it mildly. Especially the more passionate pictures . . . well, I dread it if there's one coming with Charles Farrell and Janet Gaynor . . . You, of course, will sometimes be called on to perform certain usherette duty . . . very important duty it is too . . . and what I'm saying, my lovely, is that you have to keep your eye out for certain types of behaviour . . . Some we put up with . . . other things definitely not . . . for instance . . . ' Mr Hopkins' hand went up Elsie's skirt like an oiled python.

'OOOOH!' Elsie gasped, surprise all over her face.

His hand snaked out and clamped on her breast. 'All right for us, my love, in the privacy of my office. But out there in the back row of the auditorium, definitely not. Definitely not. This too, we definitely frown on.' He gave her breast a little massage.

'But what do I do, Mr Hopkins?'

'Do? What do you do? Shine the torch on 'em. That's what you do. They'll stop soon enough. Expose 'em. An' talking about exposing, there's this . . . ' Mr Hopkins undid his fly buttons. 'See?' He looked at her with an expression bordering on indignation. 'Can't have it, my dear.'

'OOOH!' Elsie said, staring.

'Some of 'em will do this,' said Mr Hopkins, pulling her hand over to hold his erect member.

'Aaaaaah!' gasped Elsie.

Mr Hopkins stood up and fastened his fly buttons. 'Can't have it, Elsie. Never. But that's what you'll have to watch out for. But never mind that, for now. Time for your entrance.'

Mr Hopkins picked up the refreshment tray and Elsie slipped the strap around her neck.

'Not too heavy, is it?' he asked. 'Good. Now for your first appearance. Now, my lovely, walk carefully to the front of the cinema and stand level with the first row. Off you go, my girl.'

Elsie arrived at the first row of seats and waited in the centre of the aisle. The lights went up and she stood there before the packed cinema. The lights dimmed, the spotlight picked out Elsie, and a hush fell over the audience.

'SWEETS,' Elsie said in a loud clear voice. 'SOCKARUTS, CHICORETTES.'

8 *Feet First*

In mid-January of '34 Idris went from the house and didn't let his mother know where he was going. He cycled the five miles to the colliery and waited around until he got in to see the manager. He was back home in time for tea and then told his mother where he'd been.

'You're not going to work underground, and that's that,' she said. She looked shocked at the idea.

'Monday,' the boy said. 'Two and fivepence ha'penny a day.'

'No,' she said, shaking her head.

'Tommy Lewis says it's all right down there.'

'Fourteen,' she replied. 'That's what you are. Not a man yet. I decide. Not you. Whatever would your grandma say? Have you thought about that?'

The two younger children sat at the table watching the scene unfold, the boy a ten year old, the girl just a year younger. They were silent, eyes large with apprehension.

'I'll go and tell Grandma,' Idris said, obstinacy all over his face.

He left then, banging the front door as he departed.

'Eat,' she said, but the children stared at her, mouths open. 'He thinks he's a grown man. Eat now, or bed for you.'

She was an attractive woman, plumpish but shapely, the face oval, delicate almost, but the mouth was set in a hard line. 'Underground indeed,' she said in a bitter tone.

Idris had to wait to talk with his grandmother. She ran the small local greengrocery and there were a few late shoppers to see before she was free. Then, when the last of them had departed Idris told her his news.

'Starting underground on Monday, Grandma. Two an' five pence ha'penny a day. Monday. Mam said you'd have something to say about it.'

'Not I,' she rejoined, feigning surprise at the idea. 'Young man now. Fourteen. I suppose you want to bring in a few bob a week for your mother. Only natural, isn't it?'

She was around the counter now, her grey eyes appraising him shrewdly. She felt the muscles in his arm. 'Oh yes, a young man, now. Strong. I could do with a bit of help from a strong chap like you. Bit tired, I am bach. Bring in that stuff from outside. Don't think there'll be much doing now so I'll close up. All that stuff out there against the window. Potatoes, carrots, all of it. Fourpence. That's what it's worth.'

'Oh,' Idris said, delighted. 'That'll be two games of billiards at the Institute. Thank you, Grandma.'

Her hand was on his shoulder, fingers squeezing affectionately.

'Well, if you're going to be a working man you should have money to spend. Stack the stuff properly mind, and don't bruise.'

'What about Mam? She said she won't let me go.'

'Oh well, if you're determined perhaps I'll find a minute to have a word with her.' Her eyes appraised his youthful features with a keen but affectionate gaze. 'Well, I know you've thought about the risks. Not the safest job in the world. Explosions, falls, all sorts of accidents happen in the pits. Still, as I've said, if you're determined, I'll have a word with her.'

Idris finished off the chores his grandmother had set him, collected his fourpence and headed off to the Institute.

A little while later his mother and grandmother discussed the situation over a cup of tea.

'Let him,' the older woman said. 'He'll soon have enough of it. He's made up his mind. So let him try it.'

Idris's mother shook her head. 'God, what would his father have said?'

'I know. Still, Herb is dead and that's that. He can't help now. I know he wouldn't have allowed it but things would be different if he hadn't died. Idris would still be at school.'

So it was that Idris, on Monday morning, joined the group of miners waiting for the workmen's bus. It was bitterly cold, damp, and a relief to climb aboard to the comparative warmth inside but within minutes of moving off practically every one of the miners had lit a cigarette and soon Idris's eyes were running with hot tears. There was much coughing and scraping of throats, and conversations in full swing on a variety of topics. Idris was seated next to Sid Fenwick, an old school chum and he hadn't known that Sid had started at the colliery the previous week.

'Bugger this,' Idris said. 'We ought to ride our bikes.'

'I would,' Sid told him. 'But first thing in the morning it's a bit icy. 'Specially the main road.'

'Let's go the mountain road then.'

'All right. In a couple of weeks. This lot are all dying with consumption.'

'I'm glad I don't smoke.' Idris said. 'My Mam smokes and I'm not going to. Never.'

Sid was shorter than Idris, a chunky, strong looking boy, the cheek-bones high, giving the face an Oriental cast.

'Oh, I like a fag in the pictures. Park Drive. Always buy Park Drive when I go to the pictures. My mother smokes as well. So does Dad. Woodbines. My sister smokes on the sly. Our Mam says she'll kill her if she sees her smoking even though she's sixteen.'

'What's it like down there, Sid?'

'Bloody awful.'

Idris was dismayed and his mouth fell open. 'Why?'

'S'all right if you get a good butty but even with a good one it's bloody awful. I don't dislike it though.'

'You're off your head, Sid.'

'Yes, I know.' Sid turned to look at Idris. He was smiling, a daft expression on his face. 'I'm coal-crazy, see.'

'What do I do when I get there, Sid?'

'Oh, s'all right. I'll show you where to go. Got to see the overman, and gotta get a lamp. C'mon,' Sid said, climbing to his feet. 'I'll show you.'

The bus pulled up at the pit-head and the miners emerged into the chill morning air. Bright lights illuminated the road leading to the office buildings and the area around the lamp-room, and the group strode off, many of them lighting a final cigarette before starting the shift.

Sid pointed out where Idris would have to go to see the overman and gave him a friendly punch on the shoulder. 'See you when you come up, Idris.' He went off towards the lamp-room leaving Idris distinctly nervous and very much alone.

Mog Howells looked up at Idris as the youngster entered the office after a timid knock on the door.

'Idris Bowen, Mr Howells. Starting this morning.'

Mr Howells was large, running to fat, fiftyish and genial, his hair cut short and still for the most part, very dark. He appraised the youngster for a few moments. 'New talent, eh?'

Idris just stood there, uncertain of what to say.

'Don't take matches down there. 'Spect you know that though. You'll be with Dai Turner today. Just for today. Tomorrow you'll be with a permanent butty but today Dai Turner. His butty's off sick. Just do as he tells you and don't do anything silly. Watch your step down there.' He handed Idris a slip of paper. 'Take this to the lamp-room. Get your lamp and wait for me on top-pit near the cage. I'll be there in ten minutes.'

Idris collected his oil-lamp and waited near the cage for Mr Howells to arrive. He shivered with the cold as he stood watching the endless stream of miners heading into the cage, a dozen or so at a time, then disappearing from sight as the cage plunged down into the mine.

Mr Howells arrived and led him into the cage. There were a half dozen others including a couple of youngsters, not much older than Idris, and these two shrieked with laughter as the cage dropped away suddenly and Idris let out a cry of terror. His knees turned to jelly and Mr Howells gripped him around the shoulders and held him firmly.

'Shut up, you two,' Howells shouted above the whine of the cables. 'Always happens, that, first time.' he said to Idris. 'You get used to it, boy.'

Idris felt foolish, ashamed, but the others took no further interest in him and soon the cage arrived at pit-bottom with a soft bump.

They moved from the cage into the main tunnel leading to the coal face, moving aside periodically to allow the drams loaded with coal to pass them, pulled by heavy steel hawsers which whipped around dangerously as the road became uneven.

Then the coal face and Mr Howells led Idris into a stall, the roof propped up with timbers in a half a dozen places, and a heavy pungent smell which gave Idris a taste of acid on his tongue.

Dai Turner was short, bandy, and sour-looking. He was none too pleased at seeing Idris and he became truculent with Mr Howells.

'First day!' he grumbled. 'This is a fine place to put a kid on his first day. The roof's bloody treacherous, an' the work's too hard for a kid that size. Sixteen. I told you. Ought to be one about sixteen. Jesus, Mog, what are you doing to me?'

'Well, you got him Dai. Just for today. Better than no help at all. He's the only one available today. Anyway, your butty'll be back tomorrow.'

'Oh, all right. Be more bloody trouble than he's worth.'

Mr Howells departed and Dai came around the dram of muck and took a closer look at Idris. 'What did he say your name was? Idris?'

'Yes.' Idris stared fearfully at the ferocious little miner. 'Idris Bowen.'

'Right, boy, empty this dram of muck. Chuck it into the sides. Keep the big pieces for the outside. Make a wall. Here.' He handed Idris a shovel and walked away towards the coal face. He came back almost immediately. 'Don't knock into any of these posts. Be careful. Keep away from them.'

Idris removed his jacket and put it on the floor at the side of the stall. His lamp wasn't giving off much light and Dai grabbed it and stared at the low flame.

'Look at this lamp,' he said accusingly. 'What's the matter with it?'

'I don't know.' Idris replied.

'Oh Christ.' Dai's disgust was evident and he hung his own lamp from a post so they both had some light to work with. 'Well, I'll be buggered,' he grizzled. 'One bloody lamp between the two of us. Jesus, what a day this'll be.' He walked to the coal face and started to attack it with his pick. 'Bloody lamp not working,' he moaned, cutting away at the seam, and shaking his head in anger.

After they had unloaded three drams of the slag and rubble and filled them with coal Idris ached everywhere and then they stopped for a while, to eat. As they squatted at the side of the loaded dram, rats scurried about silently, bright eyes reflecting the glow from the lamp and Idris's scalp tingled with a terror he'd never known before. They were waiting for the haulier to back his horse into the stall to pull out the loaded dram and Idris threw stones at the rats but Dai told him to stop it. 'Leave 'em,' he ordered. 'If you hit one on the head and kill it, it stinks. Leave 'em. Rest.'

This was unexpected. All morning Dai had been urging Idris to greater efforts when they were loading the drams. 'Slash in, boy. Slash in. Get paid for what we load. C'mon boy, get it in there, don't waste time, and don't forget to make sure I put the number on the dram.'

More drams of muck came in to be emptied and filled with coal and Idris worked mechanically, feeling nothing he did would please Dai, and praying for the day to end. Then abruptly it was all over.

'Right that's it,' Dai said. 'Had better days, but not bad.'

Idris followed the stream of colliers making their way through the main shaft to the cage and it seemed much further than when he'd come through it on the way in. Then the cage, and the shock of the cold wind at top-pit, and Idris breathed in the fresh air and was glad to see the sky again, though it was more grey than blue.

Sid was waiting for him and Idris didn't recognise him for a few moments with his face blackened with coal-dust.

'C'mon,' Sid said. 'Let's get rid of these lamps and get on the bus.'

Idris told him about his lamp not working and Sid was all sympathy. 'I know, mun,' he said. 'You were only a couple of stalls away from us and I could hear the old bugger. Couldn't come over, no time today. Anyway, old Dai would tell me to bugger off.'

They handed in their lamps and received a brass disc with a number stamped on it. 'Tell him about that lamp,' Sid said.

Idris told the man behind the window about how the lamp hadn't worked properly all day and the man made sympathetic noises.

'Don't worry boyo. I'll see to it. Be all right tomorrow.'

They headed for the bus. 'Is it always that hard, Sid, down there?'

'Get used to it,' Sid replied. 'Builds you up, mun.'

Idris groaned in disbelief. 'What about the rats? Do they bother you?'

'Don't take no notice,' Sid replied.

'What's that funny smell down there?'

'What smell? You mean the gas. I suppose there's always gas in steam-coal pits.'

'Bloody horrible, isn't it.'

Sid nodded his agreement. 'Oh aye, it is. Horrible. Smells like bloody cats' piss.'

They were aboard the workmen's bus when Idris remembered the cigarette-smoke and already there were a dozen or so miners seated and enjoying their first cigarette since coming up from the mine.

'Oh,' he groaned, 'They're at it again.'

'Why don't you blokes put those cigarettes out?' Sid demanded.

'Cheeky young bugger,' a voice growled.

'He's jealous. Haven't got one.' someone suggested.

Eyes in black faces gave them a hostile glare. One of the men inhaled deeply and breathed out the smoke in a long sigh. 'Lovely,' he said, 'Just lovely.'

Idris walked into his home about thirty minutes later and when his mother saw him she gave a cry of anguish. 'Look at you,' she wailed. 'Black as coal, and worn out, too. Oh my God, what would your father say?'

All day Idris had worked like a man and now suddenly he became a boy. A very young boy, and he cried then, tired tears, and he told his mother about how his lamp hadn't worked properly and Dai had kept on at him all day and how the work was hard and that there were rats down there and the pit smelled like cats' piss.

'Language,' said his mother, 'and tomorrow I'm coming with you and I'll see that overman, putting you with a man like that, indeed, I'll see about that.'

At this he was mortified and ashamed of his tears and he told her she'd do no such thing. How would she get there, the workmen's bus? No indeed, he was going to have his bath, have something to eat, and he was going to the Institute for a game of billiards with the boys.

So his mother told him it was all right, and

tonight there was something special, bacon and eggs and tinned tomatoes because that was his favourite, and afterwards, pears and cream because he was a good boy and she knew he'd have to keep his strength up and then he escaped to the lavatory so he could cry in peace, but happiness now, and then when he'd had tea he was going to play billiards because now he could afford it but he'd have to borrow fourpence from Mam.

Idris bathed by the fire in the tin bath, kneeling down to wash head and shoulders first, but not the back, because miners washed the coal dust off the back only once a week because everyone knew that washing the back every day made it weak.

Then off trousers and stand in the bath and wash the rest and he was surprised how ingrained was the coal-dust after only one day, and then clean clothes on and fiddle around with the Meccano set until tea was ready. It was good when she finally cooked it, hot and steaming, and he felt tired afterwards so before going off to the Institute he followed his mother's suggestion to get a bit of rest and the next thing he knew his mother was shaking him and telling him it was time to get up.

'No,' he said, 'I won't go to the Institute yet, Mam. I can't open my eyes. I'm tired out.'

'It's too late for the Institute,' she told him. 'It's five o'clock in the morning and time to think about getting up for work.'

'What tomorrow?' Idris said in disbelief. 'It's never tomorrow.'

She assured him it was indeed tomorrow and after she went down to get him a bit of breakfast and pack something for his lunch he slid wearily from the bed and went down to the kitchen. His mother gave him a dish of porridge and a poached egg and soon he was off to catch the workmen's bus.

'I had a thirty break at snooker last night,' Sid told him when he boarded the bus. 'Never played so good.'

'I fell asleep after tea and didn't wake up till half an hour ago,' Idris replied in a disgruntled tone.

'Yes, I've done that,' Sid said. 'Makes me feel like death warmed up. Like as if you get too much sleep.'

'My mother put on a turn when I got home. Screamed when she saw me all blacked up.'

'Oh, Christ, don't remind me. When I went home after my first day my mother had a bloody great banner over the front door and half the women in the street there waiting for me. I went around the lane and went in the back way but they made me go out and look at it.'

'A banner?' Idris stared, knowing how embarrased Sid must have felt. 'What was on it?'

'What do you think? Welcome home, Sid.' Sid shook his head at the recollection. 'They're bloody daft these women. 'Specially mothers.'

'I wonder who Mr Howells will put me with

today?' Idris said. He was dreading another day with Dai Turner.

'You'll be all right today. Arnold's butty is being moved. I told Arnold about you. He's my butty's brother. Got the next stall. They're nice blokes.'

Idris's spirits lifted immediately. 'Oh, is that right, Sid? Shall I ask Mr Howells?'

'No. I'll see Arnold when we get to top-pit and he'll see Mog.'

'Oh, that would be good, Sid. I'd be in the next stall to you.'

They waited at the lamp-room for Sid's butty, Harry, and the brother, Arnold, to appear. Sid examined Idris's lamp with a professional eye.

'Don't shake it about,' he advised. 'Looks all right to me.'

'I better go and see Mr Howells,' Idris said anxiously.

'No. Here they are. Wait a bit. I hope Arnold remembers. I did tell him about you.'

The two men approached, identical specimens, lean and wiry, and smiling as they walked up to the boys.

'This is Idris, Arnold,' Sid said. 'Are you going to have him with us?'

Arnold was in his late twenties, the elder of the two brothers by a couple of years. He studied Idris for a few moments then led him off to the office. 'C'mon, let's see the boss.'

He tapped on the door and walked in. 'Morning Mog,' he said to Mr Howells. 'Got this bloke fixed up with anyone else? I'll have him with me if you like.'

Now Mr Howells studied Idris. 'Aye, young Mr Bowen. Yes, you take him then, Arnold. I think he's a willing lad. He was with Dai Turner yesterday. I'll bet he enjoyed that. Wasn't in too good a mood either, Dai. Yes, that'll be all right, Arnold.'

So it was that the day started well for Idris and the morning passed quickly, the work no less hard, but the easy-going attitude of his butty made things much more tolerable. Then, soon after they'd stopped for a bite to eat a dull, muffled crash of rocks hitting the floor and a thin scream of agony echoed along the coal-face and Idris stiffened in terror.

Arnold gripped Idris's shoulder. 'Stay where you are,' he snapped. He ran off then, along the coal face into the next stall and Idris could hear him shouting at his brother.

'Where's that come from?'

'Dai Turner's stall, I think,' Harry yelled. They ran on towards Dai's stall and Idris waited in the silence which followed. Sid came in a few minutes later.

'They're taking Dai out. Broke his back.'

'Did you see it, Sid.'

'No. Harry came back and told me. Bloody terrible, innit?'

Idris was scared and he drank some tea. He felt guilty about it being Dai Turner. He looked up at the roof. He could feel it pressing down on him.

'Will he be all right?' Idris asked the question knowing full well Dai Turner would die.

'Dunno. Harry says it was bad. Missed the most of it and one piece of rock caught him as he was bending over a dram. Could have cut him in two. He won't last, Idris. Poor bugger.'

Arnold returned to the stall and told Sid to go back to work.

'They've taken him out,' Arnold said. 'Poor chap, he caught a bad one there.' He shook his head. 'Poor old Dai.'

They worked on until the end of the shift, quiet now, except when conversation was necessary, and Arnold kept stopping to make close inspections of the roof. Just before they knocked-off for the day the haulier came into the stall and told Arnold that Dai Turner had died on the way out.

'Didn't make it to the cage,' the haulier said. 'Poor old Dai. Very sad, Arnold, but a release if you ask me. Not much future with your back smashed up like that.'

'Poor man,' Arnold said, his head shaking from side to sde. 'Jesus, what a way to go.'

'Never had any luck, Dai. You know Johnny Turk had him during the war?'

'I heard something about it. Wasn't he a sailor at one time?'

'Yes. Aye that's right enough. Stoker, really, on a tramp steamer. Was in some port or another

out East and the Turks captured the port and
poor old Dai was a prisoner for the duration. Got
treated pretty rough. They're not famous for
being gentle, the Turks. Bastards. Worse than the
Jerries by a long way. Yes, poor Dai, he had it
rough. Then to die like this.'

Like all boys growing up in the thirties, Idris
had heard plenty of stories about the war. He
could well understand how four years with the
Turks could make a man's disposition less than
agreeable. He felt a sense of guilt about Dai and
tried to think about other things.

They were sitting together on the bus when
Sid gave Idris a nudge. 'Hey,' he said, his voice
barely more than a whisper, 'Yesterday, I saw my
sister . . . naked.' He held his hands out in front
of his chest. 'Cor, she's got some tits on her.'

Idris was embarrassed. 'Will you shut up, Sid.'
He gazed out into the bus trying to find something of interest to focus on.

Sid chuckled, knowing he'd shocked Idris. 'Big,'
he said. He made a gurgling sound in his throat.

Idris blushed easily. He forgot his face was as
black as coal, that his embarrassment would go
unnoticed. He squirmed in his seat and felt like
strangling Sid.

At home, he didn't mention Dai Turner, but
told his mother he was with a new butty who was
very nice. Preoccupied with getting tea for the
children she didn't notice he was quiet, with-
drawn. That evening he went to the Institute and
played a couple of games of billiards with

Tommy Lewis. Tommy was a black-haired, squat-shaped fifteen-year old, who had already worked underground for almost twelve months.

Tommy was playing a shot when the attendant, a stern, middle-aged lady, called out to him.

'No smoking over the table if you please. Number seven, I'm talking to you. Put that cigarette in the ash-tray, IF YOU PLEASE.'

Tommy walked away from the table, took the cigarette from his mouth and put it on an ash-tray. 'All right, missus,' he replied. 'Just an oversight, see. Thank ew ever so much for calling my attention to it. Gettin' over-excited I was. One hundred break you spoiled there,' he added under his breath.

She gave him a brief, malicious glance, before returning to her novel. Tommy returned to the table, played his shot and missed.

'I'd like to go in off her,' he growled. 'Silly old bag.'

When they finished the game they sat at the side of the table watching a couple of other youngsters playing.

'You heard about the accident today?' Idris asked.

'I heard.' Tommy replied.

'I worked with him yesterday.'

'Did you? Well, you were lucky you didn't work with him today.'

'The haulier said he was a prisoner in the war. In Turkey. Had a hard time.'

'Now he's dead. Poor bugger.' Tommy shook his head, sadly.

There seemed nothing more to say about it and Idris slid from the seat and told Tommy he was going home. Tommy walked to the door with him and when they were outside he said casually: 'Don't let it worry you Idris. One in a million chance. One in a million.'

Idris slept badly that night, Dai Turner's angry face before him, scolding, nagging and shouting to Idris, 'Slash in, boy, slash in.'

The following morning he told Arnold he hadn't slept well because he'd kept thinking about Dai, and Arnold assured him that he hadn't slept too well himself, either, and Idris felt a little better then, but they both worked rather poorly during the shift, Arnold seeming to spend quite a lot of time checking the roof.

When they were going home on the workmen's bus Sid wanted to tell him some more about his sister but Idris told him to shut up, but Sid laughed and told him he was too young anyway.

The days passed by, shift following shift, and the colliery enjoyed a good run of regular work, being 'on-stop', the phrase used for not working on any particular day, quite a rarity. Idris became hardened to the demands of the job and Arnold was a fine man to work with. Idris was far from perfect, being something of a chatterbox, and he and Sid did their share of larking about when the opportunity presented itself. But they both worked hard and seldom took risks, the memory of Dai Turner's tragic end was too fresh in their minds for anything foolish.

At the end of each shift the main shaft was thronged with miners heading for the cage and Idris and Sid occasionally took an alternative route, an old disused tunnel, a long winding path to pit-bottom, to avoid the congestion. After one frightening experience they no longer came that way unless both lamps were operating properly.

Idris had gone through another day when his lamp was malfunctioning. It finally went out altogether before the end of the shift. Then Sid came along and headed off towards the old tunnel with Idris, lampless, following behind. They were about half-way through to the cage when Sid, spotting a rat a few yards ahead, gave chase, stumbled, and his lamp jolted and the flame dropped to almost zero. Darkness engulfed them and Sid shrieked in alarm. He stood still and slowly the flame returned to normal. Idris was scathing, Sid contrite, and they both knew it had been a narrow squeak. Being lost in the old tunnel without a light could well have had tragic consequences. They headed off, careful now to reach safety without further incident.

Now they no longer came to work on the bus. With the arrival of better weather they cycled or walked over the mountain road, fooling about on the way, enjoying the fresh air, talking the whole time about all the things which interested them. They discussed their respective skills at

billiards and snooker, who had scored the high-
est break, rugby, the local soccer team, Jack
Petersen, how many drams of coal they filled the
day before, and Sid talked about a girl who'd
given him 'the eye'.

They were heading home after work one day,
young bodies wearied after another shift at the
coal face, breathing in the mountain air,
approaching a cottage where an elderly woman
stood at the gate, watching them.

'Shwmai Missus,' Sid said as they drew abreast.

'Shwmai bach,' she replied.

They passed her and she called out to them.
'Hey, boys.'

They stopped and looked back at her.

'How long you two been working down
there?' she wanted to know.

'Oh, my Dad got me the job for a Christmas
present,' Sid told her.

She looked at them, her eyes sorrowful. 'What
I always says is when you go down there you
never know if you're going to come up feet first.'

'Oh,' Sid replied, laughing. 'Nice talking with
you Missus.'

They walked on and Sid looked at Idris and
said: 'Silly old cow.'

Idris said nothing but the woman's words
brought to the surface fears he had suppressed
for the past few weeks. After they cleared the
mountain road and were coming down the last
part of the lane leading to the houses he gave Sid
a nudge with his elbow.

'She's right though, Sid. Isn't she?'

'Who is?' Sid wanted to know. 'Who? The old girl back on the mountain? 'Course she's right. I just don't like people reminding me. Feet first! That's a nice thought to take to bed.'

Then just before they parted Sid looked at Idris, pointed at himself and said: 'I'm going to join the Army when I'm a bit older. That's the life, Idris. India, China. Gor, I can just see me a Bengal Lancer. Or a pilot in the Air Force.'

Sid made a buzzing sound and piloted his bomber past the Cut-Price Stores. 'BZZZZZZ ... BANG ... CRUNCH CRUNCH ...'

Idris laughed. 'Daft bugger. You can barely ride a bike.'

Then, they were coming through the old tunnel again, a Friday in late May, footsteps echoing dully, the lamps throwing crazed shadows along the sides, rats scampering as they approached.

They were half-way to the cage when the explosion blasted through the mine to give the valley its blackest day on record. From behind them an ear-splitting roar which sent shafts of terror searing into their minds and they fell to the floor in panic and fear. Another explosion followed and now dust poured into the old tunnel, and the acrid stench was overpowering. Then the roof began to fall in hundreds of places and they screamed out their terror and sobbed for their mothers to help them.

When the rumbling, roaring devastation settled down to occasional rock-falls and the sounds of scurrying rats there came intervals of silence like the pauses between the verses of hymns, except for the sobs of the two boys, relatively unharmed, but with minds numbed with shock.

Idris couldn't believe they still had light, but there it was. His own lamp was out, the flame completely gone, but miraculously Sid had shielded his lamp throughout the whole ordeal. Idris rose and pulled Sid to his feet. They linked arms and headed out towards the cage, the lamp barely penetrating more than a yard or two ahead through the heavy dust. Then a rock fall barred the way and they stared in disbelief at the pile of rubble which had crashed down and poured into the tunnel, completely sealing it off, and Idris shook his head in anguish as Sid emitted a wail of despair.

But Sid recovered quickly. He gripped Idris's arm, then pointed back towards the coal face. 'Link road,' he said. He curved his fingers to the right, indicating they would go back to the link road which connected the old tunnel with the main shaft. No need to go all the way to the coal face, but too close for comfort perhaps, but what choice had they? Idris nodded agreement and they headed back, dreading the prospect but knowing there was nowhere else to go.

They were cautious, apprehensive as they progressed towards the link road, Sid protecting his lamp, nursing it, as they scrambled over rock falls, dreading the thought that the lamp could die on them at any moment.

At last they were through to the devastated main shaft and they threaded their way past upturned drams, occasionally freezing in their tracks as above them the roof creaked and groaned and threatened to bury them. Then, a fall, a bad one and they climbed up and over it with precious little head-room to spare and at the other side, from far along the tunnel, a light.

It was their first human contact since the explosion and a disappointing one it turned out to be. Two miners, Bill Watkins, the haulier, and a collier, Jack Martin, a nice, friendly chap from further along the coal face, lay at the side of the dram-rails. Between them a lamp, the glow from which illuminated yet another fall, the rubble and boulders piled high towards the roof.

The boys knelt down to look at the two men. Bill held a finger to his lips then pointed to the roof. 'Quiet now, boys. Might be more up there ready to come down.'

'Where's the horse?' Sid wanted to know.

'Under the last fall you crawled over.'

'Oh God!'

'It would have been quick,' Bill said. 'But my leg's broken. Crawled this far. Can't get over that lot.' He jerked a thumb in the direction of the fall.

'What about Jack? He doesn't look too good.'

'Aye, I know. Been quiet like that for quite a bit. It's his thigh. Fractured.'

'We're not waiting around here, Bill. We're

going to pull you up and over that lot.' Sid was taking charge. He pulled off his jacket then unbuttoned his shirt and removed it too. 'I did quite a bit of first-aid in the scouts.' He was tearing the shirt into strips and dropping them at his feet.

'Don't worry about me, boy,' Bill said. 'I can stand being pulled over but Jack couldn't. It's bad when it's the thigh. Main bone, see.'

Idris found a length of wood and broke it in two. 'This is a bit rough, Sid.'

'I'm not looking to see if there's any bone sticking out,' Sid told them. He put the strips of wood on Jack's leg and told Idris to hold them whilst he tied them in place. 'That'll do. C'mon, let's get out of here.'

'Hey boys,' Bill said softly. 'That old horse of mine saved my life. First time he ever kicked out. First time. Kicked me yards. I was just behind him when it happened, the explosion. He kicked, and I went flying, and the roof dropped on him.' Bill shook his head. 'Good job no night shift tonight. Could have been worse.'

The youngsters dragged Jack's inert body to the foot of the fall.

'Gently, boys. Take your time.'

The boys took a fresh hold under Jack's shoulders when Bill spoke again. 'Don't expect too much when you get over that lot. I think there's a big fall between here and the cage, otherwise they'd have been back here looking for survivors.'

Idris groaned but Sid didn't seem perturbed. 'C'mon,' he said, and they started up the slope, heaving Jack after them, up into the dust-filled gap at the top, and finally the descent on the other side with rocks rolling down with them until they finally arrived on level ground, gasping for breath, spitting out the thick dust. It took all their courage to retrace their steps but back they went after depositing Jack at the side of the tunnel.

Bill groaned in agony as they pulled him up the slope and dragged him over the top of the fall but they wouldn't stop, a panic gripping them to get through to the safety of the other side.

When they were through and had finished a few minutes coughing and spitting and the burning sensation in their lungs had eased somewhat Bill insisted they move on. 'I can crawl, so leave me. Take Jack. Get a hundred yards on, away from this lot.'

'Jack's so quiet,' Idris said. 'Is he going to last?'

'Shocked,' Bill told him. 'Happens like that. Pain, see. Knocks 'em out.'

The youngsters heaved Jack up and headed off with him. Twenty yards on they caved in, exhausted. Bill crawled up to them and told them to go on ahead. 'He's a dead weight,' he said. 'You go on. Get help. Leave us.'

The boys hesitated. 'Get going, then,' Bill said gently.

They moved off towards the cage, fear enveloping them again but the shaft was clear for hundreds of yards, then ahead, sounds, voices, and soon, as they rounded a bend, bright lights danced in the distance, and their footsteps quickened and little sobs of relief escaped their lips.

Arnold was waiting for them. He stood, hands on hips, watching their approach, and soon he was embracing them, almost crying with relief.

'Oh, I thought you two was done for. Didn't think you had a hope. But we're not out yet. That's a bad 'un.'

Arnold jerked a thumb over his shoulder and the boys stared at the fall ahead. There were a couple of dozen men there, working away, passing the stones back along a line, feverishly trying to break through to the other side.

Idris told Arnold about the haulier and Jack Martin waiting for help and Arnold nodded, then gently pushed them to the side of the shaft.

'Rest boys,' he said. They sat down and watched as Arnold called to a few of the men and went off down the tunnel. Arnold's brother Harry arrived and sat down with them. He put an arm around Sid's shoulder and studied him closely.

'Thought I'd lost you, boy. Where you been? Fooling about again, I bet?'

'Aye,' Sid said ruefully. 'Bloody 'eroes we are, butty.' There were tears rolling down his cheeks now, and Harry laughed.

'Well, I always said that. That Sid, I always said, he's a bloody hero.'

'We were in the old tunnel,' Idris said.

Harry shook his head. 'Good God!'

'Do they know we're here?' Idris wanted to know.

'Aye. They know. There's a gang on the other side trying to get us out. Shouldn't take long now. Be out inside an hour.'

Arnold and the others who had gone off to bring in the two injured miners were returning, grunts and gasps heralding their arrival as they staggered over the last few yards. Simultaneously excited cries came from the men working at the fall. Then the unmistakable voice of Mog Howells calling out: 'How many of you there, boys?'

'One too many. Me.' A voice responded.

'About thirty, Mog,' another voice shouted. 'Get a move on. I'm late for tea.'

Now, a kind of delirium swept over them and there followed a bout of shaking of hands, back slapping, and cries of 'Well done, Mog.'

A cool clear night greeted them at top-pit, and hundreds of people gathered near the area of the cage cheered as each group emerged and relatives and friends rushed forward to embrace them.

Bill, the haulier, was being helped into an ambulance. He gripped Mog's arm. 'Listen Mog, those boys, Sid and Idris . . . they saved our bacon, Jack and me. After they pulled us over that fall . . . an' that took a lot of guts, there was another cave-in. We would have probably been under it. Thought I'd let you know.'

When Sid and Idris came up they were taken to Mog's office. The overman sat on the edge of his large desk and looked at them. Sid, shirtless, had a blanket around his shoulders. Mr Howells looked stern. When he spoke his voice was gruff.

'I want you boys to know,' he said, 'that I'm very proud of you. Very proud indeed. Always remember that. Right, off you go.'

They walked from the office and outside, Sid's father, his face pale and drawn, stood waiting for them.

'You all right, boys?'

Sid walked towards him and as he embraced his father the tears flowed and Sid sobbed out his relief. After a few moments he stood back and glowered with anger. 'I thought we wouldn't get out of there alive, Dad. We been bloody terrified.'

'Aye, so have I, son. So have I.'

Is my mother here?' Idris wanted to know.

'Yes. She's here, boy. I've got her in my car. She's just about off her head.' Sid's father put his arms around them and led them away. He said: 'C'mon, let's get home.'

Fatigue was overtaking the two boys and they trudged wearily towards the car. Inside, on the back seat, Idris's mother waited, her face deathly white, the features taut.

'Look at you,' she stormed as Idris climbed in alongside her. 'You obstinate little sod! I told you not to go down there. Bloody pits, they're all the same. If they don't kill you off in one go they wear you out before you're thirty. It wasn't enough they killed your father, you had to go down there as well.'

'Easy now, Mrs Bowen,' Sid's father said, soothingly. 'Anyway, I don't think he's listening.'

Idris's head was resting on his mother's shoulder and her arm went around him, her voice soft, caressing. 'Oh, my little love, I was so worried about you.'

Idris sighed and closed his eyes. Just before he fell asleep he said: 'No, no Mam, I'm not going down there again. It's feet first.'

9 *Hot Line*

'Reed's Car Hire. Can I help you?'

'Yes please, now Saturday, two o'clock, to Bedwellty chapel, marriage, will want one car, perhaps two depending.'

'Oh! Isn't that you, Bronwyn?'

'Yes, it is Bronwyn. That's you, is it, Dick?'

'Yes Bronwyn. this is Dick. Who's getting married then?'

'I am.'

'You are?'

'Yes, I am.'

'But . . .'

'I know, still, that's it, isn't it?'

'I don't know what to say.'

'Don't say nothing then.'

'Oooh . . . ! Just listening to your voice . . . I want you Bronwyn, want you . . . !'

'I want you, Dick.'

'Oh, dear dear. Tst, tst, tst, dew dew. Hang up, there's a good girl.'

'I can't hang up Dick. I have to make arrangements.'

'I'd better write it down.'

'Yes, you better. Saturday. Two o'clock. Bedwellty chapel. Marriage. Will want one car, perhaps two. Depending.'

'Wait a bit . . . Bedwellty chapel . . . Miss Pugh . . . one car . . . perhaps two . . . depending . . . Saturday . . . two o'clock . . . marriage . . . there, . . . Oh, Bronwyn lovely, what am I going to do?'

'Well Dick, you could try your wife.'

'Oh, lovely, how could you say that to me? I'm besotted. You don't think I'm wicked, do you?'

'No, never. Not you, Dick.'

'Could you see me tonight, Bronwyn? Tonight? Same time, same place? I'll have the car.'

'I'm busy, you know, Dick. Arrangements.'

'I know, I know. Arrangements. Have to be done. I know.'

'All right then, Dick, my lovely. See you then.'

'Oh, there's good, that is. I can't wait. Oh, by the way my love, who are you marrying?'

● ● ● ● ●

'Hello, is that Reed's Car Hire Service?'

'Speaking.'

'That's you, Dick, is it?'

'Yes. Is that you, Bronwyn?'

'Yes Dick. Bronwyn speaking.'

'Oooh, my lovely. Busy here. Can't talk long.'

'Something important to tell you, Dick. Very

important. Got to cancel the arrangements made previously, wedding car, Bedwellty chapel, two o'clock, Saturday, marriage.'

'Oh, what's the matter then, lovely?'

'Emlyn. Saw us. Mountain road, eight o'clock last night.'

'Ohwoo . . . What did he say, Emlyn? And how, that's what I want to know?'

'He's going to kill you Dick, and there it is. Was out rabbiting, saw your car, that's that.'

'Oh, dear dear. You can't do nothing round here. Nothing's private.'

'So please cancel car for marriage. That is convenient, is it Dick?'

'Oh, certainly. Indeed yes. I'll do that straight away. Can . . . cell . . . ation . . . wedding . . . car . . . Miss Pugh . . . Bedwellty chapel . . . Saturday . . . two o'clock . . . marriage . . . off. That's it then, Bronwyn, cancelled. I've entered it in the book.'

'Thank you, Dick.'

'What a nuisance Bronwyn after you made all the arrangements.'

'Oh, Dick bach, longing to see you, I am.'

'Tonight? Same time, same place?'

'All right, Dick my lovely. Same time, same place.'

'Wait till I see that Emlyn. I'll give him what for.'

● ● ● ● ●

'Hello, is that Reed's Car Hire Service ?'

'Speaking. Mrs Reed here.'

'Oh! Er . . . I wonder if I could speak to Mr Reed, Mrs Reed?'

'Who's speaking please?'

'It's Bronwyn Pugh, Mrs Reed. I wanted to speak to Mr Reed about some arrangements, marriage.'

'Mr Reed is not available at the moment, I'm sorry. Would you care to leave a message?'

'No thank you, Mrs Reed. I'll ring back.'

'It won't do any good, Miss Pugh. He won't be back and that's that.'

'Oh! What do you mean, Mrs Reed, he won't be back? Where is he?'

'That's what I'd like to know, Miss Pugh. He's gone off. Absconded. Eloped. Done a moonlight. With a woman, Miss Pugh. Another woman.'

'Another woman! Mr Reed? Absconded?'

'Yes Miss Pugh. Absconded, the dirty waster. And good riddance to bad rubbish. He's no great loss I can tell you. He wasn't much of a lover, Miss Pugh. Well, to put it in a nutshell, Miss Pugh, you could have put it in a nutshell.'

'Absconded!'

'I don't know what you're crying for, Miss Pugh. I'm sure I appreciate the sympathy but the rotten waster took all the money, too, and I'll have to go to the bank and borrow.'

'Oh, dear dear, Mrs Reed. I booked it and cancelled it and now I want to book it again. Booked it Monday, cancelled Tuesday, one car or two, depending, two o'clock, Bedwellty chapel, marriage. Mr Emlyn Morgan, bachelor, Miss

Bronwyn Pugh, spinster, no confetti by request. Reception Sidoli's cafe, 4 p.m., no dogs. Mr Vickery, grocer, to propose the toast, bride given away by her father, Mr Alf Pugh, miner, Gelligaer. Bridesmaids two, Miss Annie O'Keefe and Miss Florence Nott.'

'Oh, well then, that's done it, Miss Pugh. Apart from the money the waster took the best car and you'll want two and we've only got one. Sorry Miss Pugh.'

'Oh, never mind, Mrs Reed. It's only just around the corner. We'll walk.'

10 *Pick of the Bunch*

Star Window Cleaners had the Emporium con-
tract and it took up most of Monday each week.
Dave and Ronnie started at about eight a.m. and
worked through till lunch-time. Then they carried on until about two o'clock when Hugh
joined them. Hugh's job on Mondays was the
houses near the park, big houses most of them,
and he had his work cut out to get through them
by two o'clock, but Dave played up if he was late
getting to the Emporium.

Now it was well after two o'clock and Hugh
had just arrived. He didn't seem anxious to get
going with the others and messed around a bit,
rinsing out chamois leathers, changing the
water, pushing the cart to a different position.
Dave came down the ladder and spoke to him.

'For Chris'sake what are you mucking around
for? C'mon, let's get this lot finished.'

Hugh shook his head. He didn't seem himself,
somehow.

'What's the matter? You sick?'

'No.'

'What then?'

'Something happened.'

'What? What happened?'

'In number three. I only did number one. Started on three, didn't finish.'

'What! Didn't finish number three? What about five, seven and nine?'

Hugh shook his head. He was young, almost twenty, a neat build, sturdy. 'The girl there,' Hugh said.

'What? The maid? What about her?' Dave was getting impatient. He was middle-aged, thick set, a short squat man. His hair was reddish, but greying now and thinning at the temples.

'No. Not the maid. She wasn't there. The girl. The daughter.'

'Oh!'

'She was there.'

'Well, she's on holiday from school. Goes to a boarding school. Gloucester somewhere.'

'Yes. She said that. Boarding school.'

'Well, what about her? Christ, she's only about twelve.'

'Thirteen.'

'Oh, you seem to have had a nice chat. No wonder you didn't finish the other houses.'

Hugh stood at the side of the cart, fiddling with the leather. He sighed, then dropped the leather into the water.

Dave stared at him, perplexed. 'Well, are you

going to get on with it?' He handed Hugh the bucket of water and duster. 'Do the big window near the railings. Outside only. We've done inside. C'mon. Hurry up.'

Hugh held the bucket for a few moments then lowered it gently to the ground.

'She was parading around in a little nightie,' he said.

Dave's eyes narrowed and he held his breath momentarily. 'Oh,' he said.

Hugh licked his lips. 'A big girl,' he murmured.

'Go on.' Dave's voice was barely audible.

'And when I went inside she didn't exactly hide. She gave me a cup of tea.'

'Nobody else there? Just you two?'

'Nobody else. Just her. And me.'

They were on the pavement, traffic moving on the road behind them, people passing, the town busy with shoppers.

'You shouldn't have gone inside. The maid does inside. I've told you. Don't go inside when there's a chance of trouble.'

'She gave me a cup of tea. That's when I went in. I could see through her nightie. We went to the bedroom. Afterwards I choked her.'

Dave stared, and his mouth opened. He shook his head and his hands went to his hips. They stood facing each other, Dave incredulous, Hugh a dazed expression on his face.

'You killed her!' Dave's voice was barely a whisper. 'You left her there, dead?'

'Dead.' Hugh replied. 'On the bed.'

Now Dave turned to the cart and stood gripping it with both hands. Ronnie came up to them, carrying a bucket, a chamois leather slung over one shoulder.

'What's this? Family conference?'

Neither of them replied and Ronnie walked on and down the steps to the basement. He returned a few moments later with fresh water in the bucket.

'I'll do the top floor now,' he said to Dave. 'They're not too bad. Shouldn't take long.'

'No,' Hugh said. '. . . I'll go up there. You finish up down here.'

'As you like, Hugh,' Ronnie said. He was young, seventeen, a dark Celtic type, stocky and strong-looking. He handed the bucket to Hugh then groped into the pocket of his dungarees for a cigarette.

'Go on Hugh,' Dave said. He fixed his gaze on Hugh and their eyes met briefly. 'Do a good job, son.'

'Yes. A good clean job,' Hugh replied. He walked away and disappeared through the main entrance. Ronnie picked up another bucket and headed for a large display window at the end of the store. He came back for a small ladder and went off with it balancing on his shoulder. Dave sat at the end of the cart and waited. He gazed out into the street, eyes half closed, face immobile.

From six floors up Hugh hurtled to the street below and Dave remained seated as the screams of passers-by, the violent braking of cars, the sounds of shocked pedestrians rushing to Hugh's side, shattered the tranquility of a Monday afternoon in High Street.

'He's dead, Dave,' Ronnie told him a few minutes later. The boy's face was ashen and his eyes wet with tears. Dave didn't seem to respond. Ronnie shook him, gripping his shoulder, repeating what he'd said. 'I'm sorry Dave. Your son is dead.'

Dave was a long time replying. His eyes found Ronnie's and he spoke softly, as if remembering something long forgotten.

'Not my real son, see Ronnie. Adopted when he was three. Just three. We picked him carefully. Saw a lot of children and when we saw him we knew he was the one. Hugh.'

Dave's eyes went off into space. His voice became bitter. 'Bloody women,' he said.

A lost, hopeless expression came over his face and he howled out his sorrow and grief, and the shoppers stood around in groups, tearfully telling each other how terrible it was.

'Just a young boy,' they said. 'He had his whole life before him.'

11 *The Power*

Mrs Dan Price was knitting a shawl. Intricate, multi-coloured, it took up most of her half of the fireplace. She worked on it in little spasms of energy, racing against time, and there wasn't much time left. Mrs Dan Price was going to die, and Dan Price knew it too, but Dan refused to admit to his wife she would soon be dead, and that was something which annoyed her.

'Now, now,' Dan would say, 'You're going to be all right now. Don't worry about it, there's a good girl.'

As she struggled for breath her eyes would look over at him with an expression bordering on contempt, and off would go her hands in another surge of knitting. 'Going to be all right, indeed,' she'd mutter.

'Click click,' Dan would say as the needles clattered away. The sound disturbed his concentration as he listened to the wireless. 'Click click click.'

Then she died. She had striven to finish the shawl but when she died it was unfinished, and after the funeral Dan put it in the spare room.

'Lost a good woman there, boy,' they said to him, because they knew Mrs Dan Price was one of the best knitters in the valley and a lot of her work had been sold to help with the family budget. Dan's two married daughters helped serve refreshments to the mourners and when they left Dan went out to have a pint of best bitter.

He returned from the pub and got himself a bit of supper. Cup of cocoa, slice of bread and butter, piece of cheese and a pickled onion.

'Very sad, boy,' they'd said to him. 'Oh, you lost a good one there.'

The house was still, quiet, and Dan experienced a strange twinge of fear at being alone.

'Just nerves, boy,' he told himself. 'Imagination.'

Dan lay in bed alone and missed the wheezing breathing of his late wife, not yet cold in the ground. Stolid and self-sufficient though he was, sleep did not come easily, and as the distant church-bell tolled out the hours his apprehension increased, until finally, exhausted, his eyes closed and he dozed fitfully.

Familiar sounds disturbed him and he awoke with a moan of terror. From the spare room came the sound of clicking knitting needles and Dan croaked out in disbelief, 'Oh, Christ Gert, you're not going to start that?'

Click click, went the needles, and a soft, wheezy voice said, 'Click, click, click.'

With his breath exhaling in a howl of horror Dan scrambled from the bed, rushed out of the room and down the stairs like a whippet out of a trap. In the safety of the kitchen he sat shivering, waiting for dawn to end his night of terror.

'You must learn to knit,' said Mrs Flo Morgan, spiritualist, medium, clairvoyant. 'Knit, boy, that's what you must do. Because you have the power. And it's not given to many.'

'Power?' said Dan. 'Which bloody power?'

'The power to contact the "other side",' she said.

'Knit!' said Dan. 'Me knit? What would I be doing, knitting?'

'You must knit, boyo, because she won't rest until you do. Finish the shawl. Finish it or she'll never leave you.'

But this was later that day, in broad daylight, and doubts about the wisdom of consulting Mrs Flo Morgan began to assail him. Dan had three pints of best bitter and two halves of mild before he went home that night, and when, in the dark of the bedroom he was disturbed again by the sounds of the clicking knitting needles he was slower to respond. For seconds he lay there listening, then panting in terror he again fled the bedroom for the safety of the kitchen, He made tea many times over during the long night and sat drinking it at the oilcloth covered table, with unsteady hands, face white as marble.

At first light he rose from his chair and walked to the foot of the stairs.

'I'll finish the shawl, Gert,' he called out. 'I'll finish the bloody thing and be done with it.'

Later that day he had his first knitting lesson from Mrs Flo Morgan, and within a week he was working on the shawl. It took over a month to finish it because he kept getting it wrong and had to keep unravelling it. Then, when it was finished he gave it to one of his daughters.

'I don't want it, Dad,' she said. 'What would I want that thing for?'

'Hide it,' he said. 'Sell it. I don't care. You have it.'

So she took it and gave it to the Salvation Army.

'It's all done, Gert,' he called out to the empty house, when he returned home. 'Done. All done. The shawl's all done, my lovely. All done. Done, done, done. Finished. Go to Jehovah and sit at His feet, my love. Go through the Gates and rest in peace.'

That night the house was quiet but Dan didn't go to bed. Since the second day after the funeral he hadn't set foot upstairs except for the time he'd rushed up in broad daylight to grab the shawl from the spare room. He sat in the kitchen and kept the stove going. It was a long night and to pass the time he started knitting a pair of socks.

'Click click click,' he said to himself. 'Click click click click.'

12 *The Fight*

The words buzzed around the classroom and then around the school. 'A fight ... a fight ... after school ... in the park ... Snowy Jones and Ginger Jenkins ... after school. Straight after school.'

It promised to be a fight to remember, Snowy Jones taking on Ginger Jenkins, older, bigger, a known scrapper and rough with it, but Snowy, stocky and blonde-headed, had been attending training sessions under the eye of Moss Davis, a noted boxing instructor.

They waited in the park, those who rushed from the school to get a good vantage point, and finally Snowy came into view, his pal, Jack Palmer, at his side, and behind them a swarm of jostling, nudging, eager boys, minds afire at the prospect ahead and puzzled adults left standing in the wake, heads turning to stare at the retreating mob.

They waited then for the appearance of

Ginger Jenkins. After about fifteen minutes, during which time Snowy performed a few limbering-up exercises, a small boy pushed his way through the ring of spectators and spoke to Snowy.

'Our kid can't come 'cos our Mam found out he was in a fight an' she won't let 'im come out.' At these tidings a groan went up from those within earshot. 'Went home to change his shoes an' he said to tell you he'll fight you tomorrow after school.'

The word ran through the crowd and they started up a chant. 'WINDY . . . WINDY . . .'

If Snowy felt any emotion he didn't show it. He shrugged, indicating to the crowd he was there and ready, and there was nothing he could do about it.

Jack Palmer handed Snowy his jacket and Snowy pulled it on. Jack was acutely disappointed about the way things had turned out. He spotted a boy in the crowd. A youngster who had been involved in a number of fights in the park. It struck Jack as the ideal solution. He called over to him.

'Hey Vince, why don't you have a go at Snowy?'

The boy stared at Jack, surprised. 'What for?' he asked.

Jack closed on him, Snowy following to hear what was being said.

'You think you're one of the best scrappers in the school. Have a go at Snowy.'

The boy faced Jack squarely, his face reflecting anger. 'I don't want to fight Snowy,' he said. 'But if you don't shut your mouth you'll be fighting me.'

'I do the fighting, Vince.' Snowy's statement was an obvious challenge.

'I don't want to fight you Snowy.'

'Snowy's expression became a little contemptuous. 'Oh well, if you're scared?'

Vince was cornered. The crowd was silent, watching him, hardly breathing. 'No, you've never scared me, Snowy.'

Snowy took off his jacket. 'Right then, let's go.'

Vince still couldn't believe it was happening. He watched as Snowy removed his jacket and handed it to Jack Palmer, noting at the same time the gloating expression Palmer was wearing.

Vince was tempted to walk over and wipe the expression from Palmer's face but looking at Snowy, keyed up and ready for action, he knew he had enough on his hands in that direction. Vince pulled off his jacket and handed it into the crowd, then hesitantly, turned to face Snowy.

Ready?' Snowy asked.

'Yes,' Vince replied. A second later he was down on the grass, sparks flying around inside his head. Snowy had feinted with a left and cracked a right-hander straight to the jaw.

Vince lay there for a few seconds then climbed to his feet. Snowy moved in and Vince went forward to meet him, and the crowd, stunned at seeing Vince knocked to the ground, fell silent. The boys came together in a flurry of punches and Vince felt a wave of satisfaction as he connected with solid blows on his opponent. Snowy didn't seem perturbed and Vince found himself down on the grass again after a smart left-handed clip to the solar-plexus.

Vince was staggered. Chiefly he was astonished at the ease with which Snowy was hitting him, then enraged at the way things were going. They were both strong, fit boys, both members of the school rugby team. They'd never been close friends but nonetheless a fairly healthy mutual respect had always been evident. Vince decided to punch it out with Snowy, not from a calculated plan of campaign, but sheer pride.

He rose to one knee, ready to resume, and the cheering started up again when it was seen that Vince wasn't beaten yet. Vince had decided to accept whatever pain this encounter would bring but he was going to win it, come what may. Then they were toe to toe, punching at each other with all the power at their disposal until Snowy, with a deft piece of footwork, sidestepped Vince and flattened him again with another right to the jaw.

Vince lay on his back. Blood trickled from his nose and blotched his chin. His bottom lip was swollen and his left eye half-closed.

'Ought to be stopped,' the Park-keeper said.

Vince rose to one knee, taking his time before rising to his feet. A man stood by, watching the fight, his expression grim. As Vince rose to one knee he walked over and knelt down by the boy.

'You've had enough, boyo.'

'No I haven't,' Vince said. 'Not yet.'

'Oh hell,' the man said. 'Listen, you've done a bit of boxing?'

'Yes'

'Well then, box him. Christ, he's too big for you to fight with. Jab. Straight lefts. Don't bloody mix it with him.'

Vince rose and advanced towards Snowy. They circled each other, more cautious now, and Snowy, fists clenched into hard weapons of destruction, moved in to end it all with powerful lefts and rights to the head but Vince swayed out of trouble and cracked Snowy in the mouth with a straight left. He didn't follow up his advantage and waited for Snowy to commit himself again.

The crowd was quiet again and the drama unfolded slowly as the boys fought their hearts out, everything else forgotten, Vince retreating, countering, Snowy staking all on his heavy punches. The fight moved slowly around the park with urgent advice from the crowd given generously to both boys.

More adults joined the crowd but none interfered to stop the fight. Snowy, frustrated at Vince's tactics tried to rush his man but Vince plastered him with accurate stabbing lefts and rights and Snowy's eyes had an angry glare. Slowly Vince gained the upper hand but moving in to finish it off found himself once more stretched out on the grass after a full-blooded smash to the jaw.

Snowy looked down at the inert figure. His hands dropped and it seemed all over, but on the ground, slowly, painfully, Vince began once more to climb to his feet. He stood up and faced Snowy. A few seconds passed then Vince started to advance. He paused, seeing Snowy's hands still dangling at his side. Snowy's face crumpled into tears of defeat and at that second Vince pitched forward on his face and lay quite still.

Slowly Snowy sank to the ground, a lost, bewildered expression on his bloodied, bruised features.

'Those boys been fightin' almost forty minutes,' the Park-keeper said.

The man who had talked to Vince didn't take his eyes from the boys on the ground. 'Good God! As long as that?'

'That boy of yours took a pasting but he kept getting up. Game kid.'

'He's not my boy,' the man said.

'But you coached him? Told him how to fight?'

'Yes. I know. The other one. The fair headed one. He's mine.'

'But you coached the other one? Gave him advice.'

'Yes, well, getting killed wasn't he?'

'And the fair one,' the Park-keeper said, 'He's yours? He's a great little scrapper. Great.'

'Aye . . . well, he had to be, didn't he? Today, I think, he fought a champion. A real champion.'

Snowy's father picked up the boys and stood them on their feet. 'Shake hands,' he ordered. He handed his son over to Jack Palmer. 'Take him home to his mother. Tell her I'm proud of him.'

'C'mon son,' Snowy's father said to Vince. 'I'll walk home with you.'

Three months later Vince had moved from the valley, his family having decided to seek greener pastures. It was almost ten years later when he returned, a bitterly cold day in late 1940, and him in the uniform of the R.A.F. With the collar of his coat folded around his neck he wandered through High Street, met one or two people he knew, and escaped the weather for a cup of coffee in the cafe across from the square. He recognised Snowy immediately. Snowy had walked in right behind him, still the same square figure, the blonde hair, and the face of a fighter. It was cold, all right, but Snowy wore no over-coat, but he did have a pair of gloves, brown leather, and around his neck a mammoth scarf with the town's rugby colours.

Vince turned to Snowy and said: 'I should have you charged with assault, my good man.'

Snowy stared for a moment, then when he recognised Vince he smiled, and there was pleasure and admiration all over his face.

'Well, well, well,' Snowy said, shaking Vince's hand for what seemed a very long time. 'Well, well, well, well. Well, well,' he added for good measure. 'I've wondered . . . wondered so many times . . . I wonder what happened to old Vince? Honest to God, boy.'

'I've still got a lump in my lip,' Vince said.

'Oh, it was some fight, all right. I ached for weeks. I think you knocked some sense into me. Thought I might make my fortune as a professional boxer but I ended up in the church.'

Snowy pulled off his scarf to reveal his clerical collar. 'Oh yes, I'm the curate at St Giles.'

Vince shook his head. 'Incredible!' he said. He opened his overcoat to reveal his own clerical collar.

'Good Lord! You're a Padre!' Snowy smiled in disbelief.

'Touche,' they said together.

13 *A Meeting of Minds*

''Ang on, I'll think of it in a minute,' Ianto said.

'Could it have been Aberbargoed?' asked Evan.

'No.' Ianto shook his head.

'Could it have been Syngennydd?'

'No . . . well it could have been. But no, I don't think so.'

'Well could it have been Fochriew? Hengoed? Ystrad Mynach? Blackwood? Bargoed?'

'None of those.'

'Rhymney?'

'No.'

'Caerphilly?'

'No.'

'Abertrydwr?'

'No.' Ianto was shaking his head.

Walter, the barman at the Workmen's Club leant over the counter and joined in. 'Could Bedwas be the place you're looking for?'

'No, no,' Ianto said. 'It's on the tip of my tongue.'

'Ebbw Vale?' suggested Walter. 'That's a pretty big place. Big for Wales anyway.'

'No, no,' replied Ianto.

'Brithdir?'

'Definitely not.'

Evan had a go again. 'Two pints of bitter, Walt, and I'll put the best brains in Wales to solve the problem.' He concentrated for a few moments then banged a fist down on the table. 'Pontypridd?'

Ianto looked sad that such a great effort had met with failure. 'Sorry Evan. Wrong again.'

'Pengam?' said Len Lewis from another table. He was lighting a Woodbine and coughed like a man ready for an early demise.

'No,' said Ianto, when he saw Len was still breathing.

Walter came around the bar carrying the two pints of bitter. 'Cross Keys, that'll be tenpence, and I bet I got it right that time?'

'Never,' said Ianto. 'No, no, no. It's on the tip of my tongue.'

'Merthyr Tydfil?'

'Sorry Walter. Failed again.'

'Wait a minute,' Evan said. 'Is it a big place?'

'Not big . . . not little either . . . now where was it?'

'Middle size . . . Well that's Treharris.'

'No.'

'Aberdare, Abergavenny, Aber banana?'

'No . . . and no . . . an' don't be funny. This is serious.'

Walter was back behind the bar. 'Last try,' he called out. 'Gelligaer?'

'No,' Ianto assured him. 'No, no, no.'

'Wait a minute. I got it.' Evan paused trium-phantly. 'Tonypandy?'

'No. Not Tonypandy.'

'I give up,' said Evan. 'Drink your beer.'

Ianto was thoughtful. 'I thought Dowlais, but no, it's not Dowlais.'

From around the room other drinkers started shouting out the names of towns and Ianto fielded them doggedly.

'Abertillery?'

'No.'

'Ynysybwl?'

'No.'

'Aberfan?'

'No.'

'Treherbert?'

'No.'

'Treorchy?'

Ianto shook his head.

'Pontlottyn?'

'No.'

'Bedlinog?'

'No.'

'Bridgend?'

'No, no, no, . . . wait a minute . . . I got it. Pontlanfraith, it was?'

Approval was muttered and nodded all around the room, 'Pontlanfraith, was it?'

'Thank God for that,' Evan said, to the accompaniment of several 'hear hears', from nearby.

'What did you want it for, Ianto?' asked Walter, over the bar.

'Oh, Evan an' me was talking, see, and it came up. What was it we was talking about, Evan?'

'God knows,' Evan replied. 'I can't remember.'

'Nor me. I can't remember either.'

A howl of disgust echoed around the club but Ianto waved them quiet.

'Hang on, boys. Fair play. Give me a minute. I'll remember . . . it's on the tip of my tongue.'

'Was it about the accident there last week?' Evan asked.

'No, no.'

'Could it have been about the rumour that they're thinking about opening a new factory there?'

'No, hang on . . . it's on the tip of my tongue.'

'A scandal concerning a councillor?' suggested Walter.

'No. C'mon, keep askin' me . . . It'll come like a flash . . .'

14 *Not in the Line of Duty*

On a warm June day in 1928 Harry Rutherford caught the bus at the town square to make his weekly visit to the Infirmary. Harry was thirty-eight, wore a navy-blue blazer and grey flannel trousers, and under his arm he carried a small brown-paper package. His hair was thick and dark but already streaked with grey. The face was strong, with deep lines and restless eyes. He climbed on to the bus, an Infirmary 'special', tossed the package on to the overhead rack and sat back for the six mile journey.

The Infirmary was situated on the mountain road. It was red-brick, three-storied, and fairly isolated. The only other buildings in the grounds were a group of huts which housed the T.B. patients.

The nurses, starched into their uniforms, were young, strong-looking girls but the long hours and tough conditions they endured showed in the lines under their eyes.

Harry walked through the reception area and headed for the stairs. He reached the first floor and entered a large, airy ward, at the extreme end of the East Wing. Wide, double doors, swung easily at his touch, and over the doors the painted sign said: British Legion Ward.

He nodded pleasantly to a few of the patients then stopped at a bed where a man sat at the edge, gazing down dejectedly.

'Well, here we are again, Jimmy,' Harry said brightly. 'Guess what I've got in here. New set of Draughts. A nice new set.'

'Gaaah,' Jimmy replied, not looking up. He coughed and cleared his throat with a painful scraping sound. Harry stood there for a few moments, waiting.

'Don't know why you bother,' Jimmy said, his tone surly.

'Lovely out today, Jim. Thought you might be sitting outside.'

'Yaaah,' Jimmy growled. 'Stuck in here . . . an' that lot . . .' He gave a contemptuous wave around the ward. '. . . miserable sods.'

'Oh, they're not so bad, mun. Live and let live. C'mon, set 'em up. Set the Draughts up. You beat me last week. I want my revenge. I'll go and have a quick chat with the boys, then I'll be back.'

Harry walked off. He stood at one of the beds looking at a patient, a man with a bandage skull-cap and a half-empty sleeve in the right arm of the flannel pyjamas. The man waved to Harry and the sleeve flapped around.

'Hey, Sarge, come here a minute.' The face was animated, the eyes bright, eager. 'Hey, listen. She's not coming today. Bloody good job too. It's that fancy man, see. I know he's always prowlin' around the grounds waitin' for visitin' to finish. But today she's over in Ponty visitin' that cow of a mother of her's.'

Harry gave the man a bar of chocolate. 'Here you are, Davy.'

'Oh, bloody hell. Rations, is it? Better than corned beef, ennit?'

'Yes. Better than the old bully. More nutritious. Put it in the drawer, Davy. Have it tonight when you're listening to the wireless. Just take it easy, boy. Oh, look who's coming to see you? Your mother's here, Davy.'

The old lady, dressed carefully in her best black dress with a cameo brooch on the lapel, walked slowly down the ward.

'Good afternoon, Mr Rutherford,' she said respectfully.

'Nice to see you, Mrs Davies,' Harry said warmly. 'Davy's not looking too bad?'

Her eyes clouded as she looked at her son. 'No. Not too bad, I suppose.'

She sat down at the bedside and groped into her handbag. 'Sweets,' she said.

Davy held the bag of sweets in his hand and stared at them. 'Oh, rations again, is it?'

She looked weary. 'It's getting hot out there,' she said to Harry. She shook her head slowly. 'It's a long way on the bus. My feet get swollen. The heat.'

'She isn't comin' in today,' Davy stated.

'That's right,' his mother replied. 'She's dead.'

'That's right. Dead. An' 'er fancy man. Killed in a smash. Both dead.'

Davy's mother looked at Harry. 'He never remembers. Can't remember his wife died.'

'Doesn't want to,' Harry replied. 'Take it easy, Davy,' Harry said to the man.

'Killed in a smash,' Davy said. 'What are these? I wanted toffee.'

'Too sticky,' his mother said. 'My feet are hot.' She eased the shoes from her feet and groaned a sigh of relief.

Harry moved on to another patient. He sat down and looked at the man, a chunky, full-faced, balding individual, lying flat on his back and perspiring freely.

'You're back in then, Ivor?'

'Yes, in again, Sarge. Can't get enough air. Putting the old ticker under bit of strain, doctor says.' He breathed through his mouth and talked jerkily. 'Bit better now.'

'Oh, that's good.'

'You know, Sarge, you were a lucky bugger.'

'I was, wasn't I? Charmed life .'

'Not so charmed. You've still got this.'

'What, visiting?' Harry looked around the ward. 'I'd rather visit than stay in permanently.'

'Jimmy still giving you trouble?'

'The usual. He generally cheers up after a while. You take it easy, Ivor.'

'No choice, is there? What wouldn't I give for a decent pair of lungs.'

Harry rested his hand on Ivor's arm. 'Take it easy, butty.'

Jimmy was still sitting disconsolately on the side of the bed when Harry returned.

'C'mon,' Harry said firmly. 'Haven't you even taken the Draughts out of the box? Right then.' He pulled a chair up at the other side of the bed and set up the board between them. 'Hey, turn around, Jimmy. At least take a look. A new set. Lovely. C'mon. I'll give you a game. C'mon butty. I didn't come here for nothing.'

It took quite a while to persuade Jimmy to even look at the board but finally he relented and grudgingly played a game with Harry.

After winning a few games Jimmy began to get quite animated. 'Right,' he said, 'we can see who's got all the brains round here. Set 'em up again.'

'You always did manage to beat me, but I'm improving all the time,' Harry said.

'Hey, remember that time in Paris? When we came out of the line?'

'Do I? I do, that.'

'That girl . . .?'

'Oh, in the night club, you mean. That little girl in the bar? I remember her all right.' Harry was going through a familiar old routine. 'Beautiful, mun. Petite. That's what the Froggies say. Little it means. Petite. Lovely eyes. Remember those eyes? Black, they were, like anthracite. Black and shiny. And the way she looked at you. Could have eaten you up. Yes, she really fancied you, you randy old bugger. Oh, you were a sod for the women. They always fancied you though. You always looked so innocent, didn't you?'

Jimmy was nodding now, nodding and smiling.

'Go on, admit it,' Harry said. 'That was the secret. You looked so bloody innocent, didn't you?'

Jimmy banged his fist down on the bed. 'That's right,' he agreed, shaking his head with pleasure. 'That was the bloody secret all right. I looked so bloody innocent, didn't I? They didn't know I was the randiest bloke in the valleys ... but I looked innocent all right. What was it she called me? ... her little cabbage ... I thought I was more like a carrot ... funny how things come back to you ...'

'Right then,' Harry said. 'Another game. I'll set 'em up.'

Jimmy back-handed the board to the floor, scattering the pieces in all directions. He glared at Harry, his face screwed up with self-pity. 'Then that bloody action an' the bloody carrot's gone,' he cried out tearfully. 'You shoulda bloody left us there. Stuck in here like a bloody bed-pan. No good for anything.'

Jimmy poured out a babble of abuse and a

young doctor stood near the entrance, listening to what Jimmy was saying.

He stepped into the ward and spoke sharply to Jimmy. 'Keep your voice down,' he ordered. 'Any more of that behaviour and I'll have you transferred to the huts outside.'

Harry rose and advanced on him. 'Cut it out, Doctor,' he said. 'Just leave him to me.'

The young man, taken aback, was about to assert his authority but found himself backing off as Harry's eyes fixed him with a cold, hostile stare. He departed, ruffled, and Harry returned to Jimmy's bedside.

'Cheeky bastard.' Jimmy pronounced. 'He didn't wanna mess around with you, though, boyo.'

'Just a youngster,' Harry said, soothingly. 'Let's collect the Draughts up and have a game. Only a few minutes visiting time left.'

The young doctor headed for the office of the medical superintendent. He reported the incident to his chief and expressed his displeasure at what had happened. He was sitting on the wide window-ledge and the medical superintendent sat behind his desk.

'Upset you, did it boy?' the Super asked. 'Mustn't get ruffled though. Especially by what happens in the Legion ward. Society owes them everything, and that includes turning a blind eye to what may seem eccentric, perhaps normally unacceptable behaviour.'

'But the way he put up with that abuse . . .

what are they, brothers? Good Lord, . . . there he
is. Walking down there in the grounds. That's
him, the visitor.'

'Yes. He usually walks alone for a while before
he catches the bus home.' The Super didn't get
up from the desk. 'Sometimes he weeps as he
walks around. Yet I don't think he's an emotional
man.'

The young doctor said nothing but looked at
his chief, knowing there was more to follow.

'Not brothers exactly,' said the Super.
'Brothers in arms. The war's been over for ten
years now but he always comes. Every week.
Never fails. Does what he can. There are three
of them in that ward who owe their lives to
Harry Rutherford. And not a day goes by that
they don't curse him. 1917 it was. British made a
limited attack, probing enemy positions and
were driven back. Harry Rutherford, a sergeant
then, discovers that three of his men are still out
there, wounded. No hope for them if they stay
there because apart from pockets of gas, enemy
machine gun post making things difficult. The
good sergeant went off alone. Wiped out the
machine-gun nest and four Jerries, came back
with one of the wounded, went out twice more
for the others and brought them back. He didn't
know, of course, but one was emasculated,
another, apart from being deranged was to lose
an arm, the other had been gassed.'

'You seem to know all about it, sir?'

'Oh yes. I was the M.O.'

The young doctor looked close to tears. 'God, how dreadful. I'll say one thing, sir. He certainly has a lot of guts.'

The Super smiled and nodded agreement. 'That's why they gave him the Victoria Cross.'